Economic Inequality and Policy Control in the United States

DOI: 10.1057/9781137388117.0001

Other Palgrave Pivot titles

Michelle Bayefsky and Bruce Jennings: **Regulating Preimplantation Genetic Diagnosis in the United States**

Eileen Piggot-Irvine: **Goal Pursuit in Education Using Focused Action Research**

Serenella Massidda: **Audiovisual Translation in the Digital Age: The Italian Fansubbing Phenomenon**

John Board, Alfonso Dufour, Yusuf Hartavi, Charles Sutcliffe and Stephen Wells: **Risk and Trading on London's Alternative Investment Market: The Stock Market for Smaller and Growing Companies**

Franklin G. Mixon, Jr: **Public Choice Economics and the Salem Witchcraft Hysteria**

Elisa Menicucci: **Fair Value Accounting: Key Issues Arising from the Financial Crisis**

Nicoletta Pireddu: **The Works of Claudio Magris: Temporary Homes, Mobile Identities, European Borders**

Larry Patriquin: **Economic Equality and Direct Democracy in Ancient Athens**

Antoine Pécoud: **Depoliticising Migration: Global Governance and International Migration Narratives**

Gerri Kimber: **Katherine Mansfield and the Art of the Short Story: A Literary Modernist**

C. Paul Hallwood and Thomas J. Miceli: **Maritime Piracy and Its Control: An Economic Analysis**

Letizia Guglielmo and Lynée Lewis Gaillet (editors): **Contingent Faculty Publishing in Community: Case Studies for Successful Collaborations**

Katie Digan: **Places of Memory: The Case of the House of the Wannsee Conference**

Mario La Torre: **The Economics of the Audiovisual Industry: Financing TV, Film and Web**

Piero Formica: **The Role of Creative Ignorance: Portraits of Path Finders and Path Creators**

James Carson: **The Columbian Covenant: Race and the Writing of American History**

Tomasz Kamusella: **Creating Languages in Central Europe during the Last Millennium**

Imad A. Moosa and Kelly Burns: **Demystifying the Meese–Rogoff Puzzle**

Kazuhiko Togo and GVC Naidu (editors): **Building Confidence in East Asia: Maritime Conflicts, Interdependence and Asian Identity Thinking**

Aylish Wood: **Software, Animation and the Moving Image: What's in the Box?**

DOI: 10.1057/9781137388117.0001

palgrave▸pivot

Economic Inequality and Policy Control in the United States

Mark Stelzner
Assistant Professor, Nazarbayev University, Kazakhstan

palgrave
macmillan

DOI: 10.1057/9781137388117.0001

ECONOMIC INEQUALITY AND POLICY CONTROL IN THE UNITED STATES

First published in 2015 by
PALGRAVE MACMILLAN®
in the United States—a division of St. Martin's Press LLC,
175 Fifth Avenue, New York, NY 10010.

Where this book is distributed in the UK, Europe and the rest of the world, this is by Palgrave Macmillan, a division of Macmillan Publishers Limited, registered in England, company number 785998, of Houndmills, Basingstoke, Hampshire RG21 6XS.

Palgrave Macmillan is the global academic imprint of the above companies and has companies and representatives throughout the world.

ISBN: 978-1-137-38809-4 EPUB
ISBN: 978-1-137-38811-7 PDF
ISBN: 978-1-137-38964-0 Hardback

Library of Congress Cataloging-in-Publication Data is available from the Library of Congress.

A catalogue record of the book is available from the British Library.

First edition: 2015

www.palgrave.com/pivot

DOI: 10.1057/9781137388117

Contents

DOI: 10.1057/9781137388117.0001

List of Illustrations

Figures

DOI: 10.1057/9781137388117.0002

Table

DOI: 10.1057/9781137388117.0002

1

Income Inequality in the United States Today

Abstract: *In the first chapter, I analyze the evolution of income inequality in the United States from the 1950s to present. I show that the share of national income going to those in the upper reaches of the income ladder has increased considerably over the last three and a half decades, and that explaining the change in top wage incomes, which predominately include non-financial sector CEO remuneration, is central to understanding these changes. I also explore SBTC—the theory for the increase in wage income inequality which, at least until recently, has the most support from economists and politicians. Finding SBTC lacking, I end the chapter in suspense.*

Stelzner, Mark. *Economic Inequality and Policy Control in the United States.* New York: Palgrave Macmillan, 2015.
DOI: 10.1057/9781137388117.0003.

Understanding American inequality

"Across the developed world," remarked President Barak Obama in a speech in late 2013, "inequality has increased." "[T]his increasing inequality," continued the President, "is most pronounced in our country, and it challenges the very essence of who we are as a people." Many have made similar statements. "We do have an issue of income inequality in America," admitted House Speaker John Boehner in an interview with the *Texas Tribune* in May 2014. And Americans in general are concerned. A recent Gallup Poll found that 75 percent of all Democrats and 54 percent of all Republicans are dissatisfied with the level of income inequality in the United States. But how unequal is income inequality in the United States? And for how long and by how much has it increased?

Answering these questions in detail is the first step toward understanding American inequality. However, one must also ask other questions. For example, what is driving the astronomic growth in incomes for some? Is it the result of an increase in the social worth of certain individuals relative to the rest? Such an understanding is important because it justifies extreme inequality in outcome in a political system based on equality. Past and present, many have argued that this is the case. "[W]hile the law [of competition] may be sometimes hard for the individual, it is best for the race," asserted Andrew Carnegie in the beginning of the twentieth century.[1] "I believe in a merit nation, an opportunity nation where people by virtue of their education, their hard work and risk taking and their dreams—may be a little luck," explained presidential candidate Mitt Romney at a rally in Florida in 2012, can "achieve great things." From such an understanding, there is a strong case for eliminating or severely circumscribing government intervention in labor markets. And one can easily take the next logical step, as financier Russell Sage, and claim that "to rail against the accumulation of wealth is to rail against the decrees of justice," or describe negative talk about our current level of income inequality, as Romney and many other have, as just "envy."[2]

Although ideas like those held by Romney and Carnegie command a lot of attention, there are other explanations for the dramatic rise in inequality over the last three and a half decades. Some argue the relative growth in incomes for some is the result of change in the orientation of laws and institutions, which gives certain individuals the ability to increase their remuneration at the expense of others. "The game right now in America is rigged," commented Massachusetts Senator Elizabeth Warren in 2014. "It is rigged so that those at the top keep doing better and better, and everyone else is under increasing pressure, is under increasing economic strain."[3] Others have made similar statements. "There's class warfare, all right," remarked Warren Buffet, chief executive of Berkshire Hathaway, in response to the cacophony of televised commentary about government intervention. "[B]ut it's my class, the rich class, that's making war," continued Buffet, "and we're winning."[4] Such an understanding would lead to a dramatically different political response than if changing social worth explains inequality and would open up questions about how these developments are possible in a democracy.

To deepen our understanding and better answer the question above, it is important to look into the past and analyze the long-term trends in income inequality in the United States. There is much talk at present about how our current experience with income inequality is similar to the Gilded Age.[5] Indeed, many of our Gilded Age counterparts made comments similar to those of Elizabeth Warren and Warren Buffet. "Our government has been for the past few years under the control of heads of great allied corporations with special interests," asserted Woodrow Wilson of the late nineteenth and early twentieth centuries. "[I]t has submitted itself to their control. As a result, there have grown up vicious systems and schemes of governmental favoritism... far reaching in effect upon the whole fabric of life."[6] But exactly how does the Gilded Age compare to the present? And what can we learn from it? Furthermore, it is important to look at other periods in US history like the Progressive Era, the New Age, and the years of the New Deal and the Fair Deal.[7] How did income inequality evolve during these periods and what drove these changes?

In this book, we will explore these topics in greater depth. Chapter by chapter, we will pick up each of these questions to build our understanding of American income inequality. And, in the end, we will hopefully leave with a better understanding of how our economic and political systems have worked in the past and present and how to address problems we face today. But, before we can get to these deeper issues, we have to examine the evolution of US income inequality over the last three and a half decades and explore some explanations for its increase. To this we now turn.

DOI: 10.1057/9781137388117.0003

Our current experience

Using income tax data, we can organize the adult population of the United States based on each individual's total yearly earnings from all sources (wages, bonuses, dividends, interest, capital gains, etc.), with the individual receiving the lowest remuneration on the far left, the individual earning the most on far right, and each individual in between arranged such that earnings descend steadily from right to left. We can then take the top 10 percent of the population, the 10 percent of the population lined up on the far right, and track its total income as a percentage of national income. In Figure 1.1, I display this data for the 1950s through 2012.[8] As we can see, the United States went from a relative low level of income inequality during the three decades following the World War II to an extremely high level at present.

From the 1950s through the 1970s, the share of total income accruing to the top 10 percent of all adults stayed between 32 and 36 percent. What does this mean? Roughly, one out of every three dollars generated by the economic activities of all US citizens accrued to the top 10 percent of the population. The remaining two out of every three dollars went to the rest of the population (the bottom 90 percent). This was a relatively equal distribution, and it remained more or less that way in the three decades

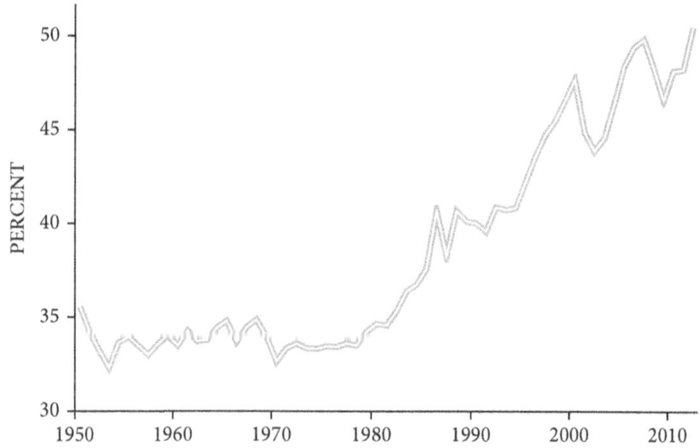

FIGURE 1.1 *Income share of top 10 percent in the United States*

Source: Piketty, Thomas and Saez, Emmanuel (2003), "Income Inequality in the United States, 1913–1998," *The Quarterly Journal of Economics*, Vol. 118, No. 1, pp. 1–39.

DOI: 10.1057/9781137388117.0003

following World War II. Thus, John F. Kennedy could rightly say in 1963 that "a rising tide lifts all boats." The large growth in national income between the 1950s and the 1970s benefited income groups equally, with the average yearly income for the bottom 90 percent of the population keeping pace with productivity growth increasing from less than $20,000 in 1950 to almost $35,000 in the late 1970s.[9]

This changed in the 1980s. Income inequality began to increase rapidly during the decade of Ronald Regan and George Bush Senior, and, except for short-term fluctuations, has continued to increase since. By the end of the 1980s, the income share of the top 10 percent had increased by more than 6 percentage points from its value in 1979. In 1988, it reached 40.63 percent of all income. This increase meant that slightly more than four out of every ten dollars generated by economic activity in the United States accrued to the top 10 percent of the population, leaving less than six out of every ten dollars for the bottom 90 percent of the population. However, it did not stop there. By the late 1990s, the income share of the top 10 percent surpassed 45 percent. And in 2012, the last year for which we have data, the top 10 percent of the population earned an equivalent of 50.42 percent of the national income. More than half of all income generated by US citizens went to the top 10 percent in 2012, and less than half was left for the bottom 90 percent of the population.

Income inequality has increased so rapidly over the last three decades that Kennedy's heartwarming metaphor is no longer true. Despite average yearly growth in output per worker of around 2 percent in the United States, the average real income of the bottom 90 percent of the US population has stagnated. In 1979, the average yearly income of the bottom 90 percent was almost $34,000. Since then, the average income of the bottom 90 percent has fluctuated between $30,000 and $37,000. However, the average over the entire period is barely more than $33,000. Indeed, during the first three years of the current decade, the average income of the bottom 90 percent was less still—barely surpassing $31,000. Income growth in the United States since the 1980s has exclusively benefited the top 10 percent of the population.

These outcomes are incredible. Indeed, the income share of the top 10 percent of the population in 2012 is the highest we have on record in the United States. In 1917, the first year we have data for this group, the income share of the top 10 percent represented 40.51 percent of the national income. During the 1920s, the share of total income accruing to the top 10 percent increased rapidly. However, by 1928, the climax of

DOI: 10.1057/9781137388117.0003

the roaring twenties, it had only reached 49.29 percent of total income—more than a percentage point less than in 2012.

A peculiar characteristic of the current increase in income inequality in the United States is that it was driven by an increase in inequality among wage incomes. What does this mean? Income can be separated into two groups: wage and capital income. Wage income comes from working and takes the form of wages, salaries, bonuses, and other payments to employees. This category includes every kind of worker, from janitors and secretaries, to managers and chief financial officers (CFOs). Capital income comes from owning financial and real assets, and takes the form of profits, dividends, interest, rents, capital gains, loyalties, and any other income stream from the ownership of an asset. The increase in the income share of the top 10 percent from between 33 and 35 percent in the late 1970s to more than 50 percent in 2012 is the result of an increase in both inequality of financial and real estate ownership and thus an increase in inequality from capital incomes, as well as an increase in inequality of wages. However, inequality of wages accounts for approximately two-thirds of the increase of the top 10 percent's share in total income over the last three and a half decades.

Skill biased technological change?

Explaining these dramatic increases in income inequality in the United States has become a hot topic in the media, in political circles, and among academics. The explanation that has received the most support from economists and politicians, at least until recently, is skill biased technological change (SBTC). The story goes as follows: since the 1980s, technological change has been concentrated in capital goods utilized by skilled workers.[10] A common example of this type of technological change is the computer and the Internet. Utilization of these technologies requires a high skill level. Thus the increase in productivity from computers, the Internet, and other similar technologies is exclusively captured by high skilled workers. As a result, business has increased its demand for high skilled workers, and because the supply of high skilled workers hasn't increased fast enough, their wages have been bided up relative to low skilled workers.

The difference between wages for high and low skilled workers has increased since the 1970s. Controlling for experience, the average hourly

DOI: 10.1057/9781137388117.0003

wage for male high school graduates in 1973 was $16.16 in the United States. By 2001, it had fallen to $10.34. On the other hand, the average hourly wage for male college graduates was $22.29 in 1973. By 2001, it had risen to $25.71.[11] If we look at the change in terms of the high–low skilled wage ratio $\left({}^{W_H}\!/_{W_L}\right)$, which is the practice in economics, we see that there was a ratio of 1.38 in 1973 and 2.49 in 2001. From this light, SBTC seems to explain the rapid increase in wage inequality.

The policy prescription for such a dynamic is simple: increase education for low skilled workers in order to increase the number of individuals who benefit from this technological change. As Claudia Goldin and Lawrence Katz explain in their recent book, *The Race between Education and Technology*, wage income inequality depends on the relative progress of education and technology.[12] If the technology that accompanies high skilled workers improves faster than low skilled workers can be educated and pass into the ranks of high skilled workers, wage inequality increases. And if low skilled workers can be educated more rapidly, diminishing the relative size of the low skilled worker pool, wage inequality decreases. Any minimum wage for low skilled workers or wage ceiling for high skilled workers would have deleterious effects on employment, growth, and education.

Although presented in a more sophisticated mathematical dress, the idea behind SBTC is not new. Speaking about the Gilded Age which spanned from the 1870s to the turn of the twentieth century—a period of increasing income inequality similar to that in which we are living today—Andrew Carnegie argued, "Individualism, Private Property, the Law of Accumulation of Wealth, and the Law of Competition are the highest results of human experience, the soil in which society so far has produced the best fruit. Unequally and unjustly, perhaps, as these laws sometimes operate," continued Carnegie, "and imperfect as they appear to the Idealist, they are nevertheless, like the highest type of man, the best and most valuable of all that humanity has yet accomplished."[13] For Carnegie and many of his contemporaries, the dramatic increase in income inequality during the Gilded Age represented the proper functioning of the market—the ascendance of great entrepreneurs uniquely able to organize men and machines and mold their activities so as to produce immense wealth for all. These men had skills that were extremely valuable in the context of the technological change that took place during the Gilded Age. As a result of the value and scarcity of

DOI: 10.1057/9781137388117.0003

these skills, their incomes skyrocketed relative to that of the average worker.

One main difference between SBTC today and ideas like those expressed by Carnegie and his contemporaries is that the latter was often tinged in a much more racist and sexist tone. Past theories similar to SBTC often went hand in hand with the theory of social Darwinism promulgated by English philosopher Herbert Spencer, and were used to justify eugenics, the manipulation of fertility through sterilization such as to reduce certain populations, and restrictions on immigration from undesirable countries. In its current form, SBTC is not presented in the same tone. However, in the construction of data used to give support to the SBTC theory, the large wage differences between African Americans and whites, and men and women, with similar experience and education levels are assumed to be the result of differences in productivity rather than institutionalized racism and sexism. To the degree that this is incorrect, and there is ample evidence of institutionalized racism and sexism, there are racial and sexist undertones in SBTC that parallel the more overt expression of the past.

SBTC is a powerful theory; explaining the astronomical increase in wage inequality as the result of individual's skills and preferences coupled with technological change helps to depoliticize the topic. It removes individuals from society and explains the large variation in outcomes based on differences in the characteristics of individuals. Laws and institutions have little role, if any, in these developments except maybe to further complicate the issue. Increasing inequality is not the result of reducing taxes on those at the upper reaches of the income ladder. Nor is it the result of the declining power of unions in the private sector and politics. Rather, it stems from the changing productivity, the changing social utility, of certain groups, and the political system would be ill advised to interfere in the process by any other means than increasing access to education for the less fortunate. Such a justification is immensely important in a society where the political system is democratic. Although never perfect in practice, democracy is based on the theory of equality. The existence of inequality in a democracy begs the question: how can an economic system that yields such unequal outcomes coexist inside a political system based on equality? The power of SBTC is that it justifies an extremely unequal economic system in a democratic society.

The debate since the 1970s has assumed that inequality is a natural and necessary result of growth, and thus, the economic system does

DOI: 10.1057/9781137388117.0003

not fundamentally conflict with the political system. "This mixture of equality and inequality sometimes smacks of inconsistency and even insincerity," concluded Arthur Okun in his classic book, *Equality and Efficiency, the Big Tradeoff*. "Yet I believe that, in many cases," Okun continued, "the institutional arrangements represent uneasy compromises rather than fundamental inconsistencies."[14] For Okun, who set the debate in economic and political circles for the last four decades, society faces a tradeoff between equality and growth and most decide to what degree its want to "compromise" growth for equality. The political system is the realm which humanizes the sometimes rough, yet always efficient economy. This debate did not stem from SBTC. Instead, SBTC was the natural explanation of wage inequality inside the context of the school of thought from which Okun was speaking.

Why is it important that the economic and political system represent a compromise and not a conflict? If SBTC or some other merit-based theory fails to explain the increase in income inequality in the United States, and thus extreme inequality is not justified on efficiency and merit, then the need for explanation multiplies. Aside from explaining the increase in income inequality in economic terms, one would have to explain why and how such an unequal outcome could persist, and indeed worsen over a period of three and a half decades, in a democracy. Such a discussion is messier than explaining outcomes as the result of relative social worth. For some, including neocons like Rick Santorum, who wants to ban the word "middle class," it is a discussion that is best avoided. However, it seems more important now than ever to have this discussion. Why? Because SBTC is not as convincing once we more critically analyze income inequality and technological change in the United States and abroad.

To only look at the income share of the top 10 percent would miss a central aspect of income inequality in the United States. The majority of the increase in income inequality in the United States has taken place at the upper reaches of the income ladder—not the top 10 percent of the population, but the top 1 percent, the top 0.1 percent and higher. In Figure 1.2, I display the income share of the top 1 percent of the population from the 1950s to present. As we can see, it stayed between 8 and 13 percent of all income from the 1950s through the 1970s. Roughly one of every ten dollars generated from economic activity accrued to the top 1 percent of the population during this period.

DOI: 10.1057/9781137388117.0003

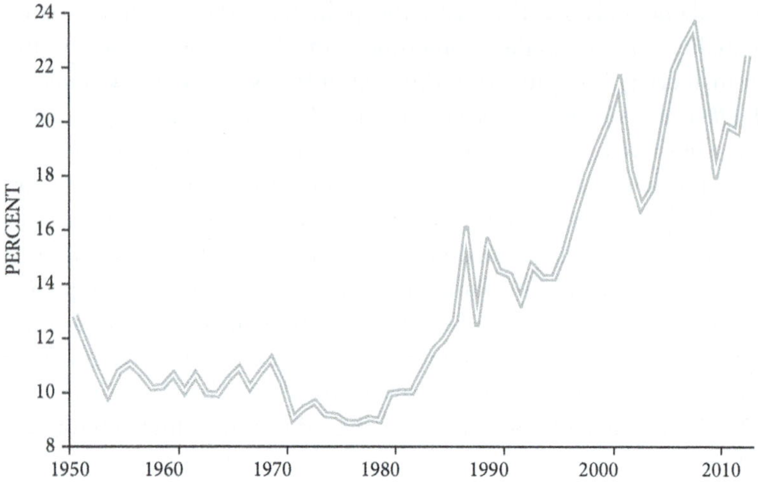

FIGURE 1.2 *Income share of top 1 percent in the United States*
Source: Piketty, Thomas and Saez, Emmanuel (2003), "Income Inequality in the United States, 1913–1998," *The Quarterly Journal of Economics*, Vol. 118, No. 1, pp. 1–39.

There was even a significant downward trend. During the 1950s, the average yearly share of the top 1 percent was just shy of 11 percent of all income. By the 1970s, this figure had fallen almost 2 percentage points, averaging just over 9 percent of all income. Like with the share of the top 10 percent during this period, these values represent a relatively low level of income inequality. However, this changed dramatically in the 1980s. The income share of the top 1 percent began to increase, and it did so more rapidly than that of the top 10 percent. By 2012, it reached 22.46 percent of all income, representing an increase of 144 percent since the 1970s.

What does this mean? If you look at the bottom 9 percent of the top 10 percent group, that is the top 10 percent excluding the top 1 percent, its experience has differed significantly from that of the top 10 percent as a whole. In Figure 1.3, I display the income share of these two overlapping income groups. As we can see, the share of the bottom 9 percent of the top 10 percent increased from around 24 percent in the 1970s to around 28 percent currently—a 15 percent increase.

This is a significant change relative to the bottom 90 percent of the population who saw their share of total income fall dramatically. However, it is miniscule compared to the astronomical increase in the

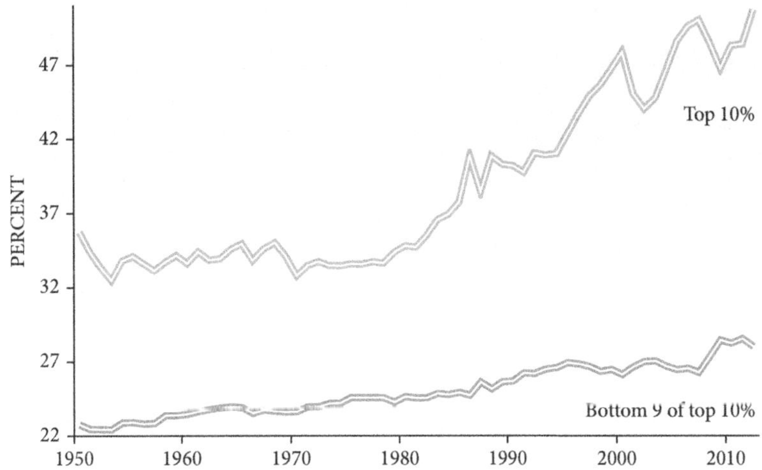

FIGURE 1.3 *Income share of top 10 and bottom 9 percent in the United States*
Source: Piketty, Thomas and Saez, Emmanuel (2003), "Income Inequality in the United States, 1913–1998", *The Quarterly Journal of Economics*, Vol. 118, No. 1, pp. 1–39.

income share of the top 1 percent. Indeed, the growth of the income share of the top 1 percent was so large over the past three decades that it is responsible for 78 percent of the growth of the income share of the top 10 percent. The divergence between the top 1 percent and the rest of the top 10 percent can be seen visually in Figure 1.3. The growing gap between the two series represents the increase in the share of total income going exclusively to the top 1 percent.

The unbelievable aspect of this story is that it does not stop there. The income share of the top 0.1 percent of the population, the top 10 percent of the top 1 percent, went from 2.83 percent of all income in the 1970s to 11.33 percent in 2012. Let's take a minute to let this sink in. Over the last 30 years, the income accruing to this group has increased so rapidly relative to that accruing to the rest of the population that its share of total income has quadrupled. Despite the exclusiveness of this elite group, the increase in its income share was so spectacular that it accounted for 56 percent of the growth in the income share of the top 10 percent, and 72 percent of the growth in the income share of the top 1 percent over the last three decades. To illustrate this point, in Figure 1.4, I display the income share of the top 1 percent and of the bottom 0.9 percent of the same group. As we can see by the growing gap between the two series,

DOI: 10.1057/9781137388117.0003

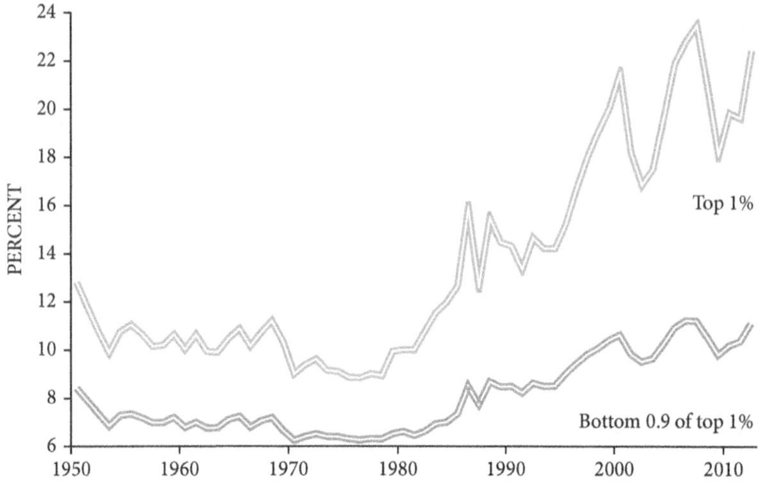

FIGURE 1.4 *Income share of top 1 and bottom 0.9 percent in the United States*
Source: Piketty, Thomas and Saez, Emmanuel (2003), "Income Inequality in the United States, 1913–1998," *The Quarterly Journal of Economics*, Vol. 118, No. 1, pp. 1–39.

the vast majority of the top 1 percent did not share in the astronomical gains made by the top 1 percent as a whole. This discrepancy represents the increase in the share of total income going exclusively to the top 0.1 percent.

If we explain the rise in inequality as a result of the relative increase in rewards to high skilled workers, how do we explain such divergent outcomes between the different groups inside of the top 10 percent? Everyone inside the top 10 percent group are high skilled workers; the ranks of the bottom 9 percent of the top 10 percent include lawyers, doctors, business owners, professors, managers, engineers, etc. Why did technological change benefit the top 1 percent and not the rest of the top 10 percent? Furthermore, why did technological change so disproportionately benefit the top 0.1 percent and not the rest of the top 1 percent? Has technological change been so biased as to reward only a tiny fraction of high skilled workers? Using SBTC to explain such developments—which are central to our experience with income inequality—seems simplistic and reaching.

As Thomas Piketty highlights in his recent book, *Capital in the Twenty-First Century*, the extreme increase in inequality in the United States over the past three decades is a direct result of the rise of supermanagers in the financial and nonfinancial sectors of the economy. One recent study found that executives at nonfinancial firms make up 43 percent of the top 0.1 percent; executives from financial firms made up 18 percent; and lawyers and real estate owners made up 12 percent. Not surprisingly, we can see the same trend in income inequality inside big firms as we can see for the nation as a whole. For example, the compensation of chief executive officers (CEOs) of Standard and Poor's (S&P) 500 companies has increased astronomically relative to their average worker. In 1983, the compensation of S&P 500 CEOs averaged 46 times that of their workers. In 1993, it reached 195, and, in 2013, the compensation of S&P 500 CEOs averaged 331 times that of their workers. CEO pay is determined by the board of directors of the company. However, CEOs appoint and set the salaries for board members and thus have considerable leverage in the determination of their own remuneration. Explaining the evolution of CEO remuneration is central to understanding the increase in income inequality in the United States. However, SBTC does not offer a convincing explanation.

Another flaw with the SBTC theory is that income inequality in many developed countries has not followed the same trend. For example, in France from the 1950s to the present, the income share of the top 10 percent of the population has fluctuated between 30 and 37 percent of all income; between the 1990s and today, its share has been stable between 33 and 34 percent of all income. If we look at the income share of the top 1 percent in France, we see a slightly different but still similar story. The share of this elite group has fluctuated between 7 and 10 percent of all income from the 1950s to today. Currently, roughly 9 percent of all income accrues to the top 1 percent in France, representing an increase since 1980. However, it is only on the order of 1 percentage point as opposed to more than 13 percentage points in the United States.

Why is this important? If SBTC is the reason for the increase in wage inequality in the United States, why is it not working in France? France is also a developed country at the cusp of the world technology frontier. High skilled workers there utilized improvements in computers, the Internet, and other technological advances. Why do we not see the same trend in France?

One might be inclined to dismiss France as an aberrant. However, it is not the only nation that has escaped dramatic increases in income inequality since the 1980s. As Piketty so thoroughly illustrates, France

DOI: 10.1057/9781137388117.0003

is actually representative of continental Europe and Japan, as well. To illustrate this point, in Figure 1.5, I display the income share of the top 1 percent excluding capital gains in Japan, Sweden, the United States, and France.[15] As we can see, in Sweden, the income share of the top 1 percent has increased since the 1980s. However, it was around 4 percent in 1980 and is only 7 percent now—still significantly below that of the United States during the 1950s, 1960s, and 1970s.

In Japan, the income share of the top 1 percent has remained between 7 and 10 percent of all income since the 1950s. Save small differences in levels, this story is the same in Germany, Denmark, Italy, Spain, and continental Europe in general. Thus, we can ask again, but this time more broadly, if SBTC is the reason for the increase in wage inequality in the United States, why is it not producing similar outcomes in other advanced industrial economies where technological change is the same? Curiously, the only other countries that have had similar, although not as dramatic, experiences with income inequality since the 1980s are the other English-speaking advanced industrial nations—Britain, Canada, and Australia. This peculiarity suggests other explanations based on shared norms and political systems.

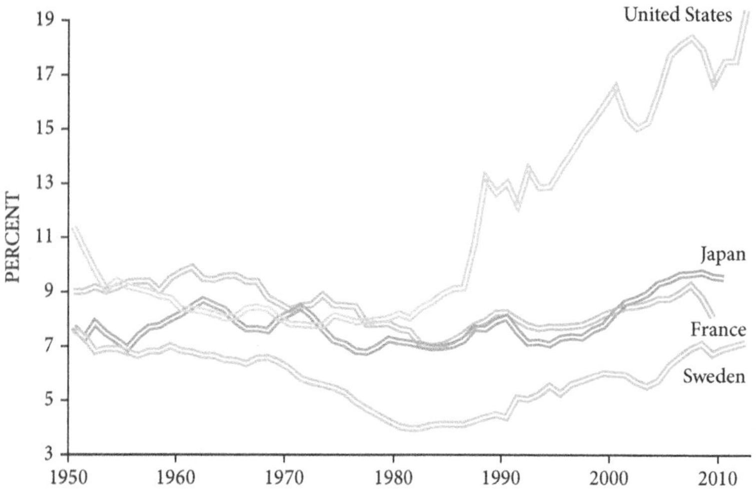

FIGURE 1.5 *Income share of top 1 percent*
Source: The World Top Incomes Database.[16]

DOI: 10.1057/9781137388117.0003

Another problem with the SBTC argument is that technology has been constantly evolving throughout the history of the United States. However, outcomes in income inequality have followed radically different trajectories during different periods in US history. For example, the newspapers in the 1950s, 1960s, and 1970s were full of concern that contemporary technological change would lead to the elimination of jobs and increasing inequality.

However, as we have seen, the income share of the top 10 percent of the population in the United States remained stable at a relative low level, and the income share of the top 1 percent actually decreased throughout this period. Why is the technological change at present different from the past? Curiously, in academic papers building cases for SBTC, the issue of technology is casually assumed—there are generally no real data to support the biased nature of productivity growth except for increasing income inequality itself. However, it is not obvious that technological change since the 1980s has been generally skill biased. For example, it seems that computer programs that check medical symptoms with databases of diseases and output diagnoses would negatively affect doctors by allowing individuals with less education to take over parts of their responsibilities. If so, this type of technological change would be biased to the detriment, not the benefit, of skilled workers.

What then is driving income inequality?

SBTC is laden with many holes, and thus seems to be a poor explanation for the rise in income inequality in the United States since the 1980s. In *Capital in the Twenty-First Century*, Thomas Piketty provides another explanation: when the return on capital is higher than growth, which he shows is typically the case, the stock of wealth grows relative to the economy. Because income from capital is more unequal than income from wages, the growing importance of wealth means that income inequality is increasing. Piketty also shows that wealth inequality and the inheritance of wealth, versus savings over the life cycle, have increased reducing the importance of merit. All of these developments bring us closer to the "patrimonial capitalism" of the nineteenth century. Although the importance of the mechanism he introduces, his meticulous documentation of historical economic series, and the clarity in which he presents the issues makes his work a classic, Piketty's main finding, as he admits, does not explain the majority of the increase in income inequality in the United States. As mentioned earlier, a peculiar, yet central aspect of the US experience is that increase in wage inequality accounts for two-thirds of the increase in income inequality over the last three and a half decades.[17] Yet, the main thrust of Piketty's book is about capital holdings and capital incomes.

As a result, the questions that we posit earlier resurface. What is driving the extreme increase in inequality in the United States? Is it possibly the result of non-meritorious forces? Why has it persisted for so long? Have we had similar experiences in the past? If so, how were they similar? How were they different? Finally, more questions surface if we find that social worth and efficiency don't explain the extreme rise in income inequality. Questions like: how has inequality coexisted in a democratic society?

In this book, we will tackle these questions to better understand and respond to issues at present. In the following chapter, we will analyze another explanation for the increase in wage inequality in the real sector in the United States since the 1980s.[18] As we will see, because of market frictions and workers' loss aversion, employers have power over employees' wages. This might seem obvious to some, but it is directly counter to the basic assumption in many mainstream economic models. Employers' monopsony powers can be countered by unions, minimum wage laws, and other types of government regulation. However, as we will see in Chapter 2, since the 1980s, laws and institutions which frame employer–employee relations have been systematically dismantled allowing business to drive a large and larger wedge between workers' social worth and what they get paid. As a result, firms have syphoned off more and more of the gains from economic activity in their favor. This increase in profits make possible, and most likely explain, increase in CEO remuneration. In Chapter 3, we will compare the current rise in income inequality and change in laws and institutions with the Gilded Age, the Progressive Era, and the New Era. As we will see, with the exception of the Progressive Era, this long period stretching from the 1870s through the 1920s has many similarities to present.

These findings beg the question of how such unequal outcomes exist in a society where the political system is based on the principle of equality. In Chapter 4, we will examine the New Deal and the Fair

Deal and look at some potential reasons we have such a mixed record of ameliorating income inequality in the United States. Finding these explanations lacking, in Chapter 5, we will look at another explanation which integrates ideas from game theory and behavioral economics and can better explain the long-term trends in the evolution of the orientation of laws and institutions and income inequality in the United States since the 1870s. Finally, in Chapter 6, we will use our new understandings to explore some ways to confront inequality at present.

Notes

1 Andrew Carnegie, "The Gospel of Wealth," The North American Review, Vol. 183, No. 599 (Sept. 21, 1906), Pp. 528–30.

2 CNN, "Romney: Income Inequality Is Just 'Envy'", January 12, 2012. For Sage quote, see Foner, E. (1998). *The Story of American Freedom*. New York: W.W. Norton. P. 139.

3 CNN, "Elizabeth Warren: Wealth Trickles Up," June 3, 2014.

4 Quoted in Stein, Ben, "In Class Warfare, Guess Which Class Is Winning," *The New York Times*, November 26, 2006.

5 The Gilded Age refers to the final three decades of the nineteenth century and the first decade of the twentieth.

6 Wilson, W., & Hale, W. B. (1913). *The New Freedom: A Call for the Emancipation of the Generous Energies of a People*. New York: Doubleday, Page & Company. Pp. 29–30.

7 The Progressive Era has roots in the nineteenth century but only got started in earnest in the second decade of the twentieth century. The New Era refers to the 1920s.

8 Unless specified otherwise, all figures and income inequality statistics quoted here include capital gains—income from the increase in the price of an asset.

9 These figures and all other figures referenced in this paper are in 2012 US Dollars, unless specified otherwise, allowing for comparison across time without distortion from changes in the price level.

10 Skilled workers usually refer to college graduates whereas unskilled workers refers to high school graduates.

11 All figures are in 2001 dollars.

12 Goldin, C. D. & Katz, L. F. (2008). *The Race between Education and Technology*. Cambridge, MA: Belknap Press of Harvard University Press.

13 Andrew Carnegie, "The Gospel of Wealth," *The North American Review*, Vol. 183, No. 599 (Sept. 21, 1906), Pp. 528–30.

DOI: 10.1057/9781137388117.0003

14 Okun, A. M. (1975). *Equality and Efficiency, the Big Tradeoff.* Washington: Brookings Institution.

15 The other series have included capital gains. As a result, these figures for the United States will be slightly lower than those in Figure 1.2.

16 For France, see Piketty, Thomas (2001). Les Hauts Revenus en France au 20ème siècle. Paris: Grasset, p. 807. Piketty, Thomas (2007). "Income, Wage and Wealth Inequality in France 1901–1998" in Atkinson, A. B. and Piketty, T. (editors) *Top Incomes over the Twentieth Century. A Contrast between Continental European and English-Speaking Countries*, Oxford University Press, chapter 3. Landais, Camille (2007). Les Hauts Revenus en France 1998–2006. Une Explosion des Inégalités? Paris School of Economics Working Paper. Series updated by Facundo Alvaredo and Thomas Piketty. For Japan, see Moriguchi, Chiaki and Saez, Emmanuel (2010). "The Evolution of Income Concentration in Japan 1886–2005" in Atkinson, A. B. and Piketty, T. (editors) *Top Incomes: A Global Perspective*, Oxford University Press, chapter 3, pp. 76–170. Series updated by Facundo Alvaredo, Chiaki Moriguchi, and Emmanuel Saez (2012, Methodological Notes). For Sweden, see Roine, Jesper and Waldenström, Daniel (2010). "Top Incomes in Sweden over the Twentieth Century" in Atkinson, A. B. and Piketty, T. (editors) *Top Incomes: A Global Perspective*, Oxford University Press, chapter 7. Series updated by the same authors.

17 Piketty, T., & Goldhammer, A. (2014). *Capital in the Twenty-First Century.*

18 The real sector is the same as the nonfinancial sector.

DOI: 10.1057/9781137388117.0003

2
Changing the Rules of the Game

Abstract: *In Chapter 2, I show that employer—employee relations changed over the last three and a half decades to the detriment of unions and labor in general. As a result, the counter balances to employers wage setting power decreased enabling business to drive a larger and larger wedge between the wage and marginal product of the average worker. The consequent increase in profits and the destruction of groups that would object to higher remuneration for those at the top made possible and probably explain the increase in CEO vis-à-vis workers' compensation in the non-financial sector. Income inequality that exists from this dynamic is not only the result of different social worth but also the result of intra-firm power dynamics.*

Stelzner, Mark. *Economic Inequality and Policy Control in the United States.* New York: Palgrave Macmillan, 2015.
DOI: 10.1057/9781137388117.0004.

In Chapter 1, we analyzed the evolution of income inequality in the United States from the 1950s to present. We found that the share of national income going to those in the upper reaches of the income ladder has increased considerably over the last three and a half decades, and that explaining the change in top wage incomes which predominantly include remuneration for CEOs in the non-financial sector is central to understanding these changes. We also explored SBTC—the theory for the increase in wage income inequality which, at least until recently, has the most support from economists and politicians. Finding SBTC lacking, we ended the last chapter in suspense. What is driving the impressive increase in income inequality in the United States since the 1980s? In this chapter, we will explore an explanation for the rise in wage income inequality in the real sector.

A shift in employer–employee relations

Shortly after taking office in 1981, President Reagan set the tone for employer–employee relations when he fired 11,400 striking air traffic controllers. The fate of the Professional Air Traffic Controllers Organization (PATCO) was an ominous warning of the dramatic changes ahead. In the aftermath, many "unions became less aggressive," explained James Peirce, president of the National Federation of Federal Employees. "If Reagan can destroy PATCO, he can destroy us, too. People didn't want to stick their neck out."[1] By late 1983, Regan's policy took a more concrete form. After a bitter battle with congressional democrats, he appointed a majority to the National Labor Relations Board (NLRB) with Donald Dotson as Chair. The general counsel and the five members of NLRB, headed by the chairman, administer and interpret the National Labor Relations Act (NLRA)—a New Deal hallmark created to protect workers' rights to bargain collectively. Because of the "open-ended ambiguity" of the NLRA, as put by one NLRB Chairman,[2] the board can reframe employer–employee relations without ever changing statute law. Writing to the American Bar Association Journal in 1980, Dotson commented: "Collective bargaining frequently means labor monopoly, the destruction of individual freedom and the destruction of the marketplace as the mechanism for determining the value of labor." Dotson's views represented a marked change for the chair of the board created to protect labor's right to bargain collectively.

DOI: 10.1057/9781137388117.0004

Moving with the winds of political change, Dotson and the other appointees rapidly reoriented the NLRB. "In only 150 days the new majority has reversed at least eight major precedents," reported *Business Week* in 1984. "By some estimates, it has already recast nearly 40 percent of the decisions made since the mid-1970s that the conservatives found objectionable." In response to one such reversal which made it possible for a firm to move production from a unionized plant to a non-union facility while its contract with the union was still in effect, Dotson explained that the NLRA "is still sound... [Instead] one of the problems in the past has been the way previous boards have interpreted it. Of course, the board can change those interpretations without having to urge Congress to change the law."[3]

Those that approved of this pro-business shift explained that it was nothing irregular. The NLRB shifted a little to the right under Republican administrations and a little to the left under Democratic administrations. However, this shift was much more dramatic. "Many of the precedents the new board has altered date not from the Carter administration but the Nixon–Ford years and before," explained the *Washington Post* in 1985. "In routine cases involving charges of unfair labor practices, moreover, the Reagan board has held for management much more than either the Carter or Nixon–Ford boards, whose records were about the same."[4] In addition to a shift in rulings, the new board decreased the effectiveness of the NLRA by allowing case backlog to increase. In his book, *Fluctuating Fortunes*, David Vogel explains that "there were 800 contested cases awaiting decisions by the full board when Regan took office; in 1984, its backlog was 1,700. The resulting bottleneck reinforced the board's anti-union "animus," as it effectively made it "much more difficult for unions to organize new workers or effectively represent the members they already had."[5]

These developments represented an effective change in labor law. The NLRA, explained Philip Sipser, a political activist and labor lawyer, no longer represents what it had in the past. "The act and the National Labor Relations Board," continued Sipser, "have become a millstone around labor's neck and create a dangerous illusion that workers, unions and the institutions of collective bargaining are protected. Nothing could be further from the truth."[6] In 1985, union leaders from Communication Workers of America (CWA) explained to the *New York Times* that the "biggest obstacle to its organizing [a Cottrell Inc. factory] was the National Labor Relations Board." The NLRB dragged its feet only slowly resolving allegations that Cottrell Inc. had illegally fired an employee active in the union drive. Mr Kiser, the union organizer, commented that "foot-dragging" by the NLRB had a "chilling effect" on Cottrell employees. "We weren't able to show the workers that they couldn't be fired," explained Mr Kiser "and that the company couldn't get away with it if they were fired." "[S]uch criticisms from union leaders," the article goes on to explain, "have become more and more frequent." An NLRB official, who asked to remain anonymous, substantiated CWA allegations. "It happens all the time," the official explained. "Typically, a company will fire the union ringleader. In the meantime, the union organizing drive is faltering, at minimum cost to the company."[7]

This reorientation of law to benefit employers did not stop when Democrats took back the White House. Early in his first term as President, Bill Clinton named William Gould and Fred Feinstein to the NLRB in hopes to slant it back to the center. However, these efforts were largely thwarted by Congressional Republicans and the two pro-business board members. In an exit interview in 1998 with the *New York Times*, Gould accused Congress of "rank interference" with the board's decisions. Speaking of the many occasions when "Congress went to bat for their corporate friends," Gould exclaimed, "I think most of us think this smacks of societies that we would call autocratic or authoritarian."

The NLRB is theoretically independent of Congress. However, Congress has a number of ways to pressure the board to adopt a policy it desires. First, Congress has to approve all candidates nominated by the President and can thus thwart a presidential nomination by denying the candidate the needed number of votes or filibustering the nomination process.[8] Conversely, Congress can put pressure on the President to nominate a candidate of its choice. Second, Congress can reduce the effectiveness of the NLRB by reducing funding to the agency. Third, Congress can use its position to put verbal pressure on the NLRB either during oversight hearings or in public venues. These strategies were all used during Clinton's time as President. Congress reduced the NLRB's funding by 2 percent in 1995 and froze funding in 1996 and 1997, forcing the board to cut its staff. As a result, delays in processing cases increased. Congress also put pressure on board members to delay key decisions until after the NLRB could be reshuffled so as to give Republican sentiments a majority. "The board has not issued decisions in many cases where he [Gould] is eager to leave an imprint," reported the *New York Times*. "Several board members wanted to delay issuing decisions until

DOI: 10.1057/9781137388117.0004

after this term ended," continued the *Times*, "in hopes that his position would no longer command a majority."[9]

These allegations seemed to prove themselves after Gould, and later Feinstein, left the board in 1998.[10] Although Clinton was able to nominate Sarah Fox to the NLRB during Congressional recess circumventing its approval, the exit of Gould and Feinstein with only one pro-labor replacement gave pro-business members a 2–1 majority. Congressional obstruction of the appointment process allowed the board to maintain this majority through Clinton's last year as President. Pivotal cases that had been filed at the beginning of Gould's term were then handled under the new majority. For example, in September 1993, *New York Post* employees went on strike because the new owner had not rehired many union employees after a buyout and had failed to honor the employees' previous contract. The strike ended after two days with a clear defeat for the strikers. The newspaper rehired less than half of the 287 dismissed union members. In response, the Newspaper Guild of New York filed a case with the NLRB for $20 million in back pay. However, this case was not decided on until November 2000—long after Mr Gould had left the board. Not surprisingly, the 2–1 pro-business majority favored the employer. Sarah Fox dissented writing that the two companies were successors and "should therefore assume ... [the] contractual obligations, among them honoring the Guild agreement."[11]

Even when cases were decided in labor's favor, they often took so long and carried such a small punishment that it was essentially a defeat. For example, union leaders filed a claim in 1997 against Smithfield Packing Company's slaughterhouse in Tar Hell, North Carolina—the world's largest pork processing plant. The union claimed that in a drive to unionize the plant the managers had fired employees because of participation in the effort, assaulted one employee for the same reason, stationed police officers at the plant on election day to intimidate workers, "illegally confiscated union materials, spied on workers' union activities, threatened to fire workers who voted for the union, and threatened to freeze wages and shut down the plant if the employees unionized."[12] The case was not decided until 2001.[13] Despite a verdict favorable for the union, the case was then tied up in appeals until 2006. Meanwhile the company was not forced to comply with the 2001 ruling even though in 2003, Smithfield was again charged with illegally firing employees for protesting. And two years later, still one year before the appeals court had reached a verdict, Human Rights Watch issued a report harshly

DOI: 10.1057/9781137388117.0004

criticizing Smithfield stating that its plants were "so bad that they violated basic human rights."[14] After all this, the 2006 decision which was in favor of the workers only forced the company to reinstate *some* of the wrongfully fired employees.[15]

The NLRB continued to slant to the right during the presidency of George W. Bush. Astonishingly, during his two terms as President, the board almost completely stopped issuing orders against employers in cases where they illegally obstructed union drives. Of 22,000 organizing drives between 1999 and 2005, "[o]nly one in five cases that filed an election petition ultimately reached a first contract," reported the *Boston Globe* in 2007. "This is despite all the cases already having shown substantial and likely majority support for representation."[16] The unsuccessfulness of the drives, explained the *Globe*, was due to illegal interference by employers without timely, or any, response from the NLRB. At the same time, as had begun under Regan, the W. Bush NLRB continued adjudicating the NLRA to the benefit of employers. In 2005, the board gave "companies greater flexibility to use a powerful anti-union weapon—locking out workers—in labor disputes," and denied non-union workers "the right to have a co-worker present when managers call them in for investigative or disciplinary meetings."[17] Given that 91.5 percent of the private sector nonagricultural labor force was not covered by a union in 2005, this decision dramatically affected employer–employee relations for a vast amount of workers. In 2006, in a verdict "praised by business," the NLRB ruled that all workers who had supervisory duties which constituted at least 10 percent of their total work time could not unionize.[18] This definition of supervisor was so broad, commented the *New York Times*, that it prohibited a huge percentage of the labor force from unionization. "Responsibilities like making out a schedule do not amount to management. If they did," reported the *Times*, "interns would be the only non-managers in many of today's workplaces."[19] These decisions further changed the rules of the game to favor employers, explained Wilma Liebman, a minority member of the NLRB. "Virtually every recent policy choice by the board," continued Liebman, "impedes collective bargaining, creates obstacles to union representation or favors employer interests."[20]

The accounts described earlier are not the exception. They represent a broad and dramatic shift in employer–employee relations that started in the early 1980s and has continued until present. In Figure 2.1, I present data on the change in frequency of certain anti-union tactics utilized

DOI: 10.1057/9781137388117.0004

TABLE 2.1 *Percentage use of certain illegal anti-union tactics*

	1986–87	1993–95	1998–99	1999–2003
Employer threats of closing plant	29%	50%	52%	57%
Workers not reinstated before election	18%	21%	23%	29%
Intensity of employer anti-union campaign (use of more than ten anti-union tactics)	0%	26%	20%	49%

Source: Bronfenbrenner (2009).

by employers. As we can see, employers have increasingly engaged in threats and other illegal methods to stymie union drives. Between 1986 and 1987, 29 percent of employers faced with union drives threatened employees with shutting down operations. Between 1993 and 1994, that figure jumped to 50 percent, and between 1999 and 2003, 57 percent of all employers faced with union drives threatened workers that they would close operations.[21]

Since the 1980s, more and more employers react to union drives in ways that would have been confined to extreme anti-union companies, like Wal-Mart, in the past. And, these extreme companies, explains Kate Bronfenbrenner, labor professor at Cornell University, have increased their use of anti-union tactics. All of this is due to the increasing "dysfunctional" and "ineffectiveness" of the NLRA and NLRB, concludes Bronfenbrenner.[22] The general trend of this change in employee–employer can be seen in the last row in Figure 2.1. Intensity of employer anti-union campaigns increased from the 1980s through the beginning of twenty-first century with only a minor decrease during the late 1990s.

As a result of congressional interference worse than that which Gould faced as chairman, the reorientation of employee–employer relations has not changed course during Barak Obama's two terms as President. "For most of President Obama's first term," commented the *New York Times*, "Republicans used legislative trickery to try to prevent the functioning of the...hated...National Labor Relations Board." Indeed, for the first 14 months of Obama's first term, the board operated with only 2 members. As a result, both the ability of the board to reach a majority decision and the number of the cases the board could handle dropped. In 2010, the Supreme Court ruled that the NLRB needed at least three members to issue decisions. This ruling opened the door to a new form of obstruction. In a half stacked board with a Democrat majority, the minority Republican member could resign or threaten to resign to

DOI: 10.1057/9781137388117.0004

thwart undesirable NLRB activity. In November 2011, this new form of minority obstruction was used for the first time. The sole Republican member of the NLRB, Brian Hayes, threatened to resign to prevent the two Democratic members of the board from issuing a decision in favor of speeding up union elections.[23] Speaking of the angry rhetoric which began the month before Hayes threatened to resign, Charles Craver, a labor law professor at George Washington University, commented that it was "as bad as it's been in terms of partisanship in the 40 years I've been in the labor field."

The effect of the reframing of employer–employee relations over the last three and a half decades can be seen in Figure 2.1 where I display private sector, nonagricultural union coverage in the United States. As we can see, between 23 and 24 percent of all private sector nonagricultural workers were covered by unions in the late 1970s. Coverage fell in the 1980s and has continued to fall since. In 1988, just over 14 percent of private sector nonagricultural workers were covered by unions. In 2000, that number fell to just under 10 percent. Currently, union coverage of private sector nonagricultural workers stands at 7.5 percent—similar to what it was before the NLRA was passed in 1935.

Although other factors have played a part in the decline of unions, their role has often been exaggerated. For example, many have argued that structural changes in our economy, the transformation from industrial to service oriented, is a major reason for the dramatic decline in

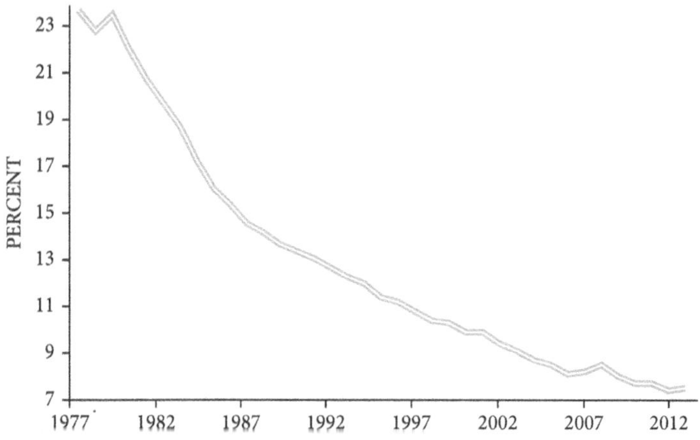

FIGURE 2.1 *Union coverage among private sector, nonagricultural workers*
Source: http://unionstats.gsu.edu/.

unionization in the United States. As our economy changed over the last three and a half decades, unions have failed to organize expanding sectors. However, comments like these seem to miss the point. The changing orientation of the NLRB, Congress, and laws and institutions in general made organization of these new sectors extremely difficult, if not impossible. The dramatic shift in unionization between the 1920s and the second half of the 1930s provides a good example of this point. From the turn of the twentieth century to 1930, the number of workers in steel, rubber, textiles, and automobiles factories jumped from under 4 million to almost 8 million. However, the large majority of these workers remained unorganized. Some contemporaries explained the inability of unions to set firm roots in these industries as the result of characteristics of the industries themselves. With the dramatic shift in laws and institutions to protect workers and empower collective bargaining in the mid-1930s, unions spread like wildfire in southern textile mills, Detroit auto plants, Pittsburgh steel mills, and Akron rubber factories.

At the same time, the decline in unionization is not the result of changing worker's preferences. Data paint exactly the opposite picture. In 1984, around 30 percent of nonunion private sector employees said they wanted a union in their workplace. In 2005, that figure increased to more than 50 percent of nonunion private sector workers.

The result

The reinterpretation of the NLRA and the reorientation of the NLRB, as intended by Donald Dotson and others, has empowered the decentralized decision-making process of the market to determine the value of labor. Contrary to their beliefs, these developments have not led us to the world where workers are paid the equivalent to what they add to production at the margin. Instead, labor market frictions and workers' own loss aversion have left them defenseless against reduction in the wage below the marginal product. The increase in profits that results has opened up the possibility for and probably led to tandem increases in remuneration for CEOs in the non-financial sector. Let's see how this works.

In mainstream economics, it is assumed that employers have no wage setting powers. Firms take the equilibrium wage from the aggregate labor market as given and hire as many workers as they want at that price. In this perfectly efficient world, workers are paid their marginal product,

DOI: 10.1057/9781137388117.0004

the increase in total production resulting from the last worker. As a result, income inequality is justified on efficiency and merit. Individuals that add more to production at the margin have higher wages, and individuals that add less have lower wages. However, the assumption that firms have no wage setting powers is unrealistic.

Extensive psychological and behavioral economics studies have shown that people are loss averse; we more negatively value losses than we positively value gains of the same magnitude. Estimates of the difference in valuation between equivalent losses and gains are surprisingly high; both experimental and natural cases have shown it to be somewhere between two and two and a half. That means that a loss of $1,000 would be valued equivalent to a gain of $2,000 to $2,500. Although peculiar, this behavioral trait has been argued to describe central outcomes in economics. For example, bond yields are consistently lower than those on the stock market. This is a puzzle: why don't investors move more of their money into the stock market to take advantage of these gains? If they did, as mainstream economists predict, expected gains from bonds and stocks would equalize. A high level of risk aversion could explain the stock–bond yield gap. However, individuals would have to be so risk averse that they would be indifferent between playing a game where they have a 50–50 chance of winning $50,000 and $100,000 and not playing the game and receiving $51,209. Instead, behavioral economists Sholomo Benartzi and Richard Thaler argue that loss aversion explains this puzzle. Stocks are much more volatile in the short run—often falling into the red. Even though on average in the long run these losses would be more than compensated yielding a higher return than bonds, individuals value the short-term loss higher than the equivalent gain.[24]

Loss averse employees would give employers a somewhat captive audience. In most cases when a worker leaves her job, she incurs losses in the short run from the decrease in pay during the job search—interview period. This is called frictional unemployment in economics. If a worker is loss adverse and has a short time horizon, she would negatively value the potential losses from leaving her job much higher than the potential gains from obtaining another job. Assuming that the level of loss aversion is slightly different for different workers, an employer would face an effective labor supply curve that is upward sloping for those individuals already at the firm. The employer could decrease the wage he pays to his employees and would only lose those workers with a small loss aversion. He could continue decreasing the wage and, still, only lose another small

DOI: 10.1057/9781137388117.0004

portion of his employees. In this setting, the wage chosen by a profit maximizing firm is less than the marginal product.[25]

This outcome would exhibit some degree of stability. Marginal product is very difficult to calculate in the real world. Workers doing the same job are not identical in abilities. At the same time, firms often have many different types of workers, from janitors and secretaries to accountants and managers. The contributions of each dramatically differs in many ways. As a result, calculating the marginal product of every worker requires oversight, and even then it is far from exact. For firms to calculate the marginal product of individuals that do not work for them is without a doubt much harder and more costly than to calculate for their own workers. Thus it is likely that firms will economize by assuming a worker's wage is a good measure of her marginal product.[26] This time and money saving strategy might be discarded when labor shortages are extreme. However, such cases are rare. Even in the late 1990s when contemporaries claimed that anyone could get a job who wanted one, unemployment, measured broadly, never went below 6.8 percent in the United States and was only below 7.5 percent for less than a year.[27]

To the extent that income inequality exists in this setting, it is not just the result of differential productivity and thus cannot be justified solely on efficiency and merit. Instead, it is also the result of intra-firm power dynamics resulting from market frictions and workers' loss aversion. Laws and institutions that empower unions or mandate a minimum wage can counterbalance employers' wage setting powers and bring remuneration closer to the marginal product. Conversely, dismantling such laws and institutions leaves workers defenseless against decreases in remuneration below their marginal product. Because CEOs' wages are paid out of profits and CEOs have considerable leverage in the determination of their own remuneration, dismantling laws and institutions that counterbalance employers' wage setting power, which is what we have seen happened in the United States since the 1980s, would lead to an increase in profits and probably an increase in remuneration for CEOs in the non-financial sector.[28] This dynamic is modeled explicitly in the mathematical appendix to the chapter.

In Figure 2.2, I graph union coverage of private sector nonagricultural workers against the income share of the top 1 percent. As we can see, there is a strong negative relationship between the two variables. When union coverage is high, income inequality is low. When union coverage is low, income inequality is high. This outcome is in complete accord with

DOI: 10.1057/9781137388117.0004

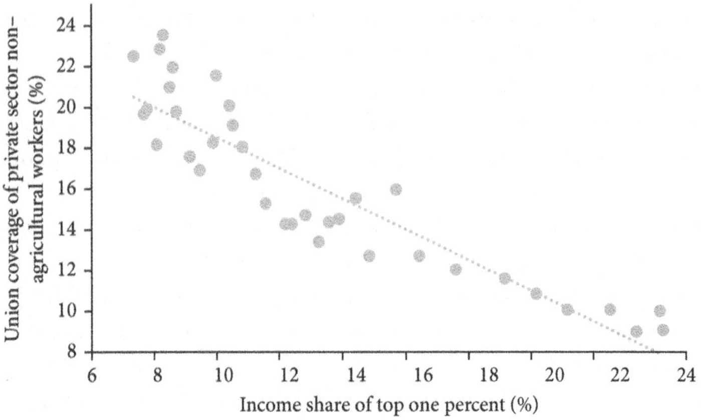

FIGURE 2.2 *Union coverage and income inequality*
Source: Author.

the theory put forward earlier and in the mathematical appendix. The dismantling of laws and institutions that protected collective bargaining led to the decline in unionization allowing employers to drive a larger and larger wedge between the wage and the marginal product. This made possible and probably explains the increase in CEO remuneration in the real sector of the economy which makes up a large part of the income share of the top 1 percent.

This sole dynamic doesn't explain the entire rise in wage inequality in the non-financial sector in the United States.[29] For example, in the stylized history earlier, we do not look at the dramatic change in taxation from the 1980s to present. To a certain degree, this omission was intentional. The income share data we analyzed in Chapter 1 are before tax income and thus point to inequality stemming from the wage setting process. However, such an exposition leaves out a key part of the story; taxation plays an important role in ameliorating or embracing inequality. Since the 1980s, tax law has been remade in the direction of embracing inequality. Average federal tax rates for the top 1 percent of income earners fell from just below 49 percent in 1970 to around 30 percent in 2004. For the top 0.1 percent, average federal tax rates dropped from around 65 percent to below 35 percent. And, for the top 0.01 percent, average tax rate fell from above 75 percent to below 35 percent. As a result, from 1980 to 2003, the degree to which taxation reduced inequality in the United States fell by more than 25 percent.[30] At the same time, the fall in tax rates, argues Thomas Piketty, have played a causal role in the increase in CEO remuneration. As top surtax rates are decreased, continues Piketty, the incentives for CEOs to increase their pay also increases. The result is higher CEO pay.[31]

These points aside, the reorientation of labor law since the 1980s seems to have played a crucial role in the increase in wage inequality in the non-financial sector in the United States. Income inequality that results from this process represents an increase in the difference between what workers produce at the margin and what they are paid. Because of the resulting increase in profits, reduction in power of groups at the firm and industry level which would resist increase in CEO pay, and nature of its determination, the remuneration for real sector CEOs is likely to increase in tandem. Inequality resulting from this dynamic is not solely based on merit but also on intra-firm power dynamics and thus opens up questions that were neatly closed by SBTC. Questions like: how can such unequal outcomes persist, and indeed worsen over a period of three and a half decades, in a democracy? But before we get to this topic, let us explore the Gilded Age, the Progressive Era, and the New Era to get a better understanding of our long-term experience with income inequality.

Mathematical Appendix

We can show mathematically the relationship between laws and institutions and the difference between what workers add to production at the margin and their wage. Let's define Δ as the difference between the marginal product and the wage:

$$\Delta = \alpha l^{\alpha-1} - W_{min} \qquad (1)$$

Equation 1 assumes that the production function is given by $q = l^{\alpha}$. q is the quantity produced, and l is the number of workers at the firm. The α term formalizes changes in productivity as the firm adds more labor. If each additional unit of labor adds the same value to the production process, α would equal 1. If each additional worker added a little less, α would be less than 1. The first term on the right side of equation 1, $\alpha l^{\alpha-1}$, is the marginal product—the increase in total production resulting from adding one more worker. ($\alpha l^{\alpha-1}$ is the derivative of l^{α} in terms of l.) The

DOI: 10.1057/9781137388117.0004

second term on the left-hand side of equation 1, W_{min}, is the marginal cost at the employment level the firm will choose. This result assumes both unions and laws mandating a minimum wage effectively create a wage floor for employers that is above the wage employers would choose when free of counterbalancing powers.[32]

If we formalize the supply curve, $w = f(l)$, and take its inverse, we can specify equation 1 in terms of W_{min}:

$$\Delta = \alpha(f^{-1}(W_{min}))^{\alpha-1} - W_{min} \tag{2}$$

As explained earlier, the supply curve facing the firm will be upward sloping due to workers' loss aversion and market frictions. At the same time, $w = f(l)$ allows for flexibility in the distribution of workers' loss aversion. $f^{-1}(w)$ is the mirror image of $f(l)$ about the $w = l$ line and thus is also upward sloping. By taking the derivative of equation 2, we can analyze how Δ will change when laws and institutions, W_{min}, change:

$$\frac{d\Delta}{dW_{min}} = \alpha(\alpha-1)(f^{-1}(W_{min}))^{\alpha-2} \cdot \frac{\delta f^{-1}(W_{min})}{\delta W_{min}} - 1 \tag{3}$$

Because $f^{-1}(W)$ and $\frac{\delta f^{-1}(w)}{\delta w}$ are always positive, equation 3 is less than 0 if $\alpha \leq 1$. If $\alpha > 1$, equation 3 is still less than 0 if $\frac{\delta f^{-1}(W_{min})}{\delta W_{min}} = \frac{(f^{-1}(W_{min}))^{2-\alpha}}{\alpha(\alpha-1)} \cdot \frac{d\Delta}{dW_{min}} < 0$ means that increasing the minimum wage or empowering unions to do the same decreases the difference between what workers add to production at the margin and what they get paid. Conversely, allowing the nominal value of the minimum wage to deteriorate or dismantling laws and institutions that empower unions would increase Δ. As we have seen, this is what happened in the United States since the 1980s.

Notes

1 Quoted in the *Washington Post*; May 31, 1987, p. A1.

2 See Gould, W. B. (2000). *Labored Relations: Law, Politics, and the NLRB—A Memoir*. Cambridge, MA: MIT Press. p. 124.

DOI: 10.1057/9781137388117.0004

3 “NLRB Ruling That Are Inflaming Labor Relations,” *Business Week*, June 11, 1984, p. 122.
4 *The Washington Post*, July 6, 1985, p. A18.
5 Vogel, D. (1989). *Fluctuating Fortunes: The Political Power of Business in America*. New York: Basic Books. p.270.
6 *The New York Times*, July 1, 1985, p. A14.
7 Ibid., July 9, 1985, p. A14.
8 In the past, this was a ceremonial process where Congress, even if controlled by the party not in the White House, approved all presidential nominations. This changed in the 1980s. Democrats thwarted Regan's first choice for Chair of the NLRB. Ironically, they won the battle but lost the war with Dotson's appointment. This was not the case for Republicans during the Clinton administration who were able to put pressure on the President and the board to bend its actions in a more desirable direction.
9 *The New York Times*, July 23, 1998, p. A14.
10 Feinstein asked President Clinton not to renominate him to the board because he feared the repercussions of House Republicans who hotly opposed him.
11 Greenhouse, Steven. *The New York Times* (1923-Current file) [New York, N.Y.] November 3, 2000: B12.
12 Ibid., May 10, 2006, p. A21.
13 Ibid., January 4, 2001, Sack, Kevin. *The New York Times* (1923-Current file) [New York, N.Y.] January 4, 2001: A18.
14 Ibid., January 26, 2005, Greenhouse, Steven. *The New York Times* (1923-Current file) [New York, N.Y.] January 26, 2005: A13.
15 Ibid., May 10, 2006, p. A21.
16 *The Boston Globe*, June 21, 2007, Kochan, Thomas A; Ferguson, John Paul. *Boston Globe* [Boston, MA] June 21, 2007: A.9.
17 *The New York Times*, January 2, 2005; p. 12.
18 Ibid., October 4, 2006; p. A16.
19 Ibid., October 7, 2006; p. A14.
20 Quoted from *The New York Times*, December 14, 2007, p. A33.
21 Kate Bronfenbrenner, “No Holds Barred: The Intensification of Employer Opposition to Organizing,” Economic Policy Institute Briefing Paper No. 235 (May 30, 2009).
22 Ibid.
23 *The New York Times*, November 22, 2011; “Republican Might Quit Labor Board.”
24 See Benartzi, S. & Thaler, R. H. (1995) “Myopic Loss Aversion and the Equity Premium Puzzle,” *Quarterly Journal of Economics*, 110, 1. (February 01, 1995).
25 Alan Manning and a number of other authors explain how frictional unemployment could lead to effective monopsony. The proposition here

expands on that by highlighting loss aversion which would dramatically increase the degree to which frictions in the labor market give employers a captive workforce. For Manning's explanation, see Manning, A. (2003). *Monopsony in Motion: Imperfect Competition in Labor Markets*. Princeton, NJ: Princeton University Press.

26 Amos Tversky and Daniel Kahneman demonstrate the number of ways human judgment is bounded under uncertainty. See Kahneman, D., Slovic, P., & Tversky, A. (1982). *Judgment under Uncertainty: Heuristics and Biases*. Cambridge: Cambridge University Press. Paul Krugman talks about the effect of this same dynamic during recessions and depression. People who are out of work for a while are considered unemployable. See Krugman, P. R. (2012). *End This Depression Now!* New York: W.W. Norton & Co. pp. 10–11.

27 By measured broadly, I mean U6 unemployment. U6 unemployment is the total unemployed, plus all persons marginally attached to the labor force, plus total employed part time for economic reasons, as a percentage of the civilian labor force plus all persons marginally attached to the labor force. See http://research.stlouisfed.org/fred2/series/U6RATE.

28 This result is shown explicitly in the mathematical appendix of this chapter.

29 Financial deregulation began around the same time Regan started to reorient the NLRB. As more and more of the Great Depression era financial safeguards were being torn down, salaries of top executives in finance dually increased. Presently, they have reached staggering levels. In 2012, the total income of the top 40 hedge fund managers and traders was equivalent to the yearly income of 300,000 school teachers, nearly one-third of all the high school teachers in the United States. Even though the correlation between deregulation and the increase in financial executives' salaries doesn't imply causality, explains Paul Krugman, Nobel Laureate in economics, it is very likely that deregulation played a key part in the increase in financial sector wage incomes. For more information, see Wages and Human Capital in the U.S. Financial Industry: 1909–2006, Thomas Philippon and Ariell Reshef. NBER Working Paper No. 14644, January 2009.

30 Hacker, J. S. & Pierson, P. (2010). *Winner-Take-All Politics: How Washington Made the Rich Richer—And Turned Its Back on the Middle Class*. New York: Simon & Schuster. pp. 48 & 52.

31 Piketty, T. & Goldhammer, A. (2014). *Capital in the Twenty-First Century*.

32 The marginal cost at wages higher than W_m would take a different form.

DOI: 10.1057/9781137388117.0004

3

The Gilded Age, the Progressive Era, and the New Era

Abstract: *In Chapter 3, I show that the period spanning from the Gilded Age through the New Era in the United States was remarkably similar to the present. During both periods, laws and institutions were oriented to embrace inequality by empowering minority groups in the economic realm at the expense of the majority. At the same time, the income share of the top 1 percent was rising, and, at the end of both of these periods or the farthest point reached during the current period, the income share of the top 1 percent reached a high in US history. Nondemocratic elements of our political system played a central during both periods.*

Stelzner, Mark. *Economic Inequality and Policy Control in the United States.* New York: Palgrave Macmillan, 2015.
DOI: 10.1057/9781137388117.0005.

In the last chapter, we found that employer–employee relations changed over the last three and a half decades to the detriment of unions and labor in general. As a result, the counter-balances to employers wage setting power decreased enabling business to drive a larger and larger wedge between the wage and marginal product of the average worker. The consequent increase in profits and the destruction of groups that would object to higher remuneration for those at the top made possible and probably explain the increase in CEO vis-à-vis workers' compensation in the non-financial sector. Income inequality that exists from this dynamic is not only the result of different social worth but also the result of intra-firm power dynamics. These developments are baffling; how is it that laws and institutions are oriented to benefit narrow segments of the population when our political system is based on equality? Before addressing this paradox, it behooves us to analyze our history. To explore such questions as: has the United States had similar experiences in the past? If so, how were they similar and how were they different? In this chapter, we will answer these questions by analyzing income inequality and the orientation of laws and institutions in the United States from the 1870s through the 1920s.

Income inequality between the 1870s and 1920s

We only have a few years of data on income shares of top earning groups before 1913—the year the current income tax was initiated. Although we cannot be completely sure of the exact trajectory year by year, we do know that income inequality between the 1870s and the 1920s was increasing. In Figure 3.1, I display the income share of the top 1 percent of all US Americans between 1866 and 1929.[1] As we can see, in the late 1860s, during the final years of the Civil War income tax, the income share of the top 1 percent averaged 9.12 percent of total income. This figure is similar to that of the late 1970s and represents a low in US history. Unfortunately, there are no data on the income share of the top 1 percent between the Civil War income tax and the current income tax. The former was allowed to expire in 1872, and, besides the short, half year of the 1894 income tax, there was no other federal income tax and thus no national data on top incomes until 1913. Consequently, we can only estimate an average trend for the missing years. The dotted line connecting the data for the nineteenth century to the data for the twentieth century represents the required average trend line for the two series to meet. This trend line should be taken as a *very rough*, first approximation of the income share of the top 1 percent from 1869 to 1912. By the time the current income tax was implemented in 1913, the income share of the top 1 percent had increased to almost 18 percent of total income, and, by 1916, it almost reached 19 percent of all income. During the late 1910s, the income share of the top 1 percent decreased reaching 14.45 percent in 1920. However, in the 1920s, income inequality shot up once again, and, by 1928, the income share of the top 1 percent of the population surpassed 21 percent of all income—a value slightly less than at present but still representing a high in US history.

What was the orientation of laws and institutions during this period? Were laws made to embrace inequality, or were they made to empower broad sections of the population? Can the theory we explored in the last chapter explain the increase in income inequality from the Gilded Age through the New Era? To be sure, the Gilded Age was the birthplace of many laws purported to be bastions of equality. The Interstate Commerce Act and the famed Sherman Anti-Trust Act were made law in the middle of this period. Both were championed as remedies for the increasing monopoly power of railroads and the other large corporations of the time. Thus, it might be that the increase in inequality we see in Figure 3.1 did not derive from the same change in laws and

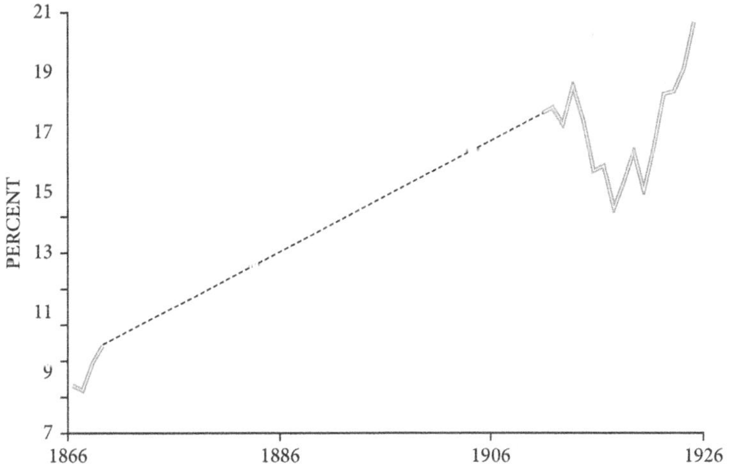

FIGURE 3.1 *Income share of top 1 percent of tax units in the United States*
Source: Author.

DOI: 10.1057/9781137388117.0005

institutions as we saw was the case from the 1980s to the present. At the same time, any keen observer of politics from any period will agree that the de facto orientation of a law does not always correspond to the statements which clothe it in political debates. Therefore, it could be that the de facto orientation of laws and institutions followed a trend similar to that of the 1980s to present even though on first appearance it doesn't seem to be the case. In order to answer these questions better, let's now turn to history.

The orientation of laws and institutions—the state level

Most of the legislation passed between the 1870s and 1920s was done at the state level. For example, laws that attempted to curb monopoly pricing and price discrimination by stipulating maximum rates railroads could charge passengers and for transporting freight and maximum rates grain warehouses could charge for storage were purely a state endeavor in the 1870s. In 1871, state legislatures in Illinois and Minnesota both passed maximum rate laws. In 1874, Wisconsin and Iowa followed suit.[2] Likewise, state legislatures in Illinois, Indiana, Missouri, New Jersey, Pennsylvania, and Ohio formed bureaus of labor in their states in the 1870s.[3] And, in the first half of the 1880s, state legislatures in California, Iowa, Michigan, New York, Tennessee, Wisconsin, and Kansas also passed legislation for labor boards. Rules regulating factory inspection were first adopted at the state level. In 1878, New Jersey's state legislature adopted the first laws mandating factory inspection, and in the next six years, five other states did the same.[4] Indeed, judged by their titles and purported purpose, state legislatures passed an impressive body of laws from the 1870s through the 1920s regarding such issues as maximum hours employees were allowed to work, child labor, weighing of coal for the determination of miner remuneration, payment in script, tenement labor, injunctions, and many other issues pertinent to labor.

Before the mid-1880s, some state laws were successful. For example, in 1871, Minnesota passed a law to reduce railroad monopoly pricing by regulating fairs. The state set up a railroad commissioner to administer its maximum rate law. Railroads that failed to comply were subject to forfeiture of charter or a fine of up to $1,000 for each violation. Contemporaries attributed the state law with some success. "[N]otwithstanding the

DOI: 10.1057/9781137388117.0005

imperfections of the law, and the fact that the companies have professed to disregard it," reported Governor of Minnesota, Horace Austin in 1872, "I am convinced that it has in no small degree, modified their charges and saved the people no inconsiderable sum, in the aggregate."[5] Other state level labor legislation saw success. Massachusetts state legislature passed a law in 1874 prohibiting women working in mills from laboring more than eight hours a day. "Because few mills, if any, could function long after the women had gone home," explains labor historian David Montgomery, "the law effectively established a new standard for [men and women in] textiles" for a time.[6]

In some instances, effective laws were repealed or replaced by ineffective laws as a result of lobbying strategies employed by those the laws sought to regulate. For example, in 1875, Minnesota's state legislature repealed its laws regulating rates for railroads and public store houses. In 1876, Wisconsin's legislature did the same. Thus, in 1877 when the Supreme Court ruled in *Munn v. Illinois* that the state had the power to regulate business when it affected a public good, many of the states which had initiated legislation that led to *Munn v. Illinois* had already repealed the laws under scrutiny. "[T]he question now definitely settled by the Court [in *Munn v. Illinois*] has, for the most part, become of little practical moment," concluded the president of the Chicago & North Western Railroad, in his annual report for 1877, "the States whose acts gave rise to this legislation having repealed their onerous laws, excepting the State of Iowa, were biennial sessions of its Legislature have no doubt longer delayed similar action." As predicted, Iowa state legislature repealed its rate laws the very next year. In its place, the legislature enacted a commission to "give advice" to the railroads in regard to rates. However, the railroads did not have to follow the advice and the commission's salaries were paid by the railroads.[7]

At the same time, many state labor laws were ineffective. Labor historian Henry David makes this point. Before 1886 with "one or two exceptions, none [of the state bureau of labors were]... equipped either in funds or personnel to function properly." In terms of child labor legislation for the same period, "It can safely be said that the age levels were so low, the means of escaping the restriction so numerous, the penalties for violation so mild, and the machinery for administration so inadequate," argues David, "that this legislation did not prevent the employment of young children in industry." Indeed, David even goes on to conclude: in general, before the mid-1880s, state laws "were seriously lacking in proper administrative provisions. There were many loopholes for escape, the inspectors were few and generally lax, and the penalties for violations were too mild. Thus, the law may give a more favorable picture of industrial conditions than was actually the case."[8]

In the South, the picture was much different. After redeeming their states from Republican control,[9] Southern Democrats remade laws and institutions so as to assert white dominance over black labor. "Broad new vagrancy laws allowed the arrest of virtually any person without a job," explains historian Eric Foner, "and 'antienticement' laws made it a criminal offence to offer employment to an individual already under contract, or to leave a job before a contract had expired." Laws were also put in place which banned the sale of unginned cotton and other farm products during the night. The intention of these laws were to increase the monopsony buying power of white southerners by reducing African Americans' freedom in selling labor and crops. Although not explicitly stated, all these laws were meant for the newly freedmen. "[A] single instance of punishment of whites under these acts has never occurred," noted a Tennessee black convention, "and is not expected." At the same time, punishment for petty theft was severely increased. In North Carolina and Virginia, "they send [a man] to the penitentiary if he steals a chicken," charged a black spokesman. If not the intent, the result was to enable the prolific growth of the convict labor system. "Within two months of Redemption," explains Foner, "South Carolina's legislature authorized the hiring out of virtually every convict in the state, as did Florida after dismantling its penitentiary." "Railroads, mining and lumber companies, and planters vied for access to this new form of involuntary labor, the vast majority of whom were blacks imprisoned for petty crimes." This process also took place outside the law. African Americans were abducted by whites; a sham trial took place in which the newly freedman or woman was coerced into signing a contract of servitude with some local businessman in lieu of formal sentencing. Although the data on this development are not good, it seems that this informal system grew as the nineteenth century progressed. Consequently, although "the region's new upper class of planters, merchants, and industrialists prospered," concludes Foner, "the majority of Southerners of both races sank deeper and deeper into poverty."[10]

After the mid-1880s, things changed outside the South. State and federal courts became much more aggressive and were able to stymie most state level legislation that seriously interfered with business. For example, in 1884, New York state legislature passed a law prohibiting the manufacture of cigars in tenement housing.[11] One year later, the New York Court of Appeals struck down the law in *In re Jacobs* arguing that it infringed on labor's constitutional liberty.[12] This decision marked a revolutionary change in the court's understanding of due process of the law, liberty, and property. Until *Jacobs*, due process was understood as a procedural guarantee. As mentioned in the declaration of independence, liberty referred to freedom from restraint, and property denoted the static right to ownership and use. *Jacobs* was the first step in completely reinterpreting these terms and the legislature's place in society. Liberty was reconstrued to mean the right to following one's lawful calling. The definition of property was expanded to include such intangibles as earning potential, and due process was reinterpreted to signify a guarantee to protection against "arbitrary" legislation which infringed on one's liberties and property.[13] This reinterpretation from *Munn v. Illinois*, which became more and more entrenched after *Jacobs*, justified court intervention to invalidate legislation, and prevent labor activity, when it infringed on citizens' newly defined liberties and property rights. Intervene they did. "During the 1880s and 1890s," explains labor historian William Forbath, "courts were far more likely than not to strike down the very laws that labor sought most avidly." Indeed, "by 1920," continues Forbath, "courts had struck down roughly three hundred labor laws."[14]

In Figure 3.2, I display an index for court activity in regard to labor laws from the 1870s through the end of the nineteenth century. The index is the sum of all state labor laws struck down by the court minus the sum of all state labor laws upheld by the court for each year.[15] A more positive value represents a situation where the courts were more aggressive in trumping state level labor laws.

A negative value represents a situation where the courts were more supportive in upholding state labor laws. As we can see, the courts became more and more aggressive in striking down labor friendly state legislation from the mid-1880s through the end of the nineteenth century.

Because the overall effect of state labor laws was ambiguous outside the South before the mid-1880s and because state labor laws came under increasingly aggressive attack from the courts after 1885, let's explore how law played out on the ground by analyzing the most important development of the period—the labor injunction. Injunctions are court orders for a specific person or group of people to cease and desist from

DOI: 10.1057/9781137388117.0005

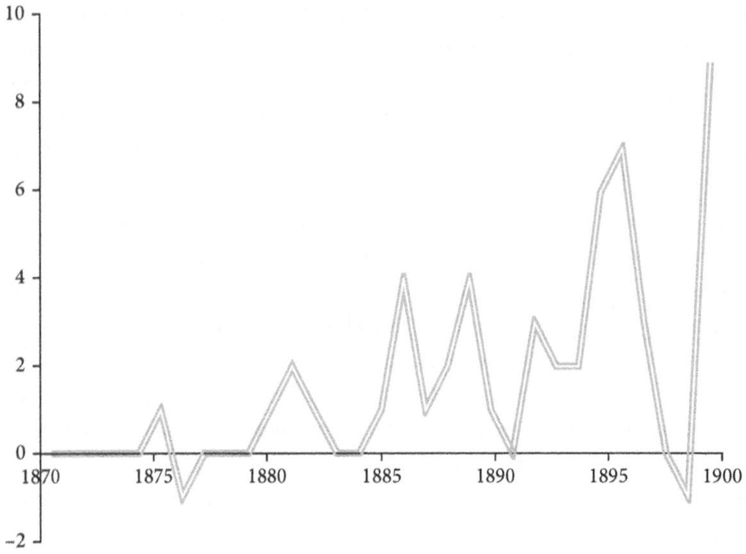

FIGURE 3.2 *Index of court activity in regard to state-level labor laws*
Source: Author.

some action. They were used during this period to stymie the collective activity of labor through the threat of jail terms and/or fines without trial by jury. The injunction did not develop through the legislative branch—although many of the late-nineteenth-century statues were used to increase its reach. It developed through the judiciary, and the legislature was either unwilling or unable (due to gridlock or inability to match the court's resolve) to resist. The injunction was most successfully and aggressively applied to strikes that utilized broad based support, sought to obtain more than just monetary gains (like a closed shop), and utilized secondary boycotts and "don't patronize" lists.[16] To a large degree, the injunction was a trump on local developments. It represented law which could be used over labor friendly local authorities to the benefit of business. To its history, we now turn.

A brief history of the labor injunction

On June 1, 1877, the Pennsylvania Railroad cut employees' wages by 10 percent. One by one, other railroads followed suit. In mid-July, in

DOI: 10.1057/9781137388117.0005

reaction to these cuts and a number of other grievances, railway workers went on strike in Illinois and Indiana. These strikes set off other strikes and mob activity in cities and towns throughout the country. At its climax, the scale of the Great Strike of 1877, as it came to be called, was immense. About 50,000 miles of the nation's 75,000 miles of track were located in areas affected by the strike, and, in a number of cities including Chicago, general strikes paralyzed all activity.[17]

The strike pitted the collective organization and wills of workers against those of the railroads.[18] During this spatter of contests, a development in law took place which tilted the playing field, for some railroads, in their advantage. Some of the struck line, like the Erie, were in receivership—the roads had failed and were in the custody of the courts. Circuit Judge Thomas Drummond of Chicago and Judge Samuel Treat of a district in Southern Illinois issued "writs of assistance"—orders to US marshals to protect the property in the custody of the court and to arrest anyone who tried to damage or interfere with its functioning. Offenders did not have to be specifically named in the writ, nor served notice of its existence, and could be punished for contempt of court without the trouble of a trial by jury.[19]

Although "writs of assistance" only played a minor role during the Great Strike of 1877, solvent railway companies couldn't help but notice how effective they were for trains in receivership. "[A]s our recent experience has shown," explained Thomas Scott, President of the largest corporation of the time, the Pennsylvania Railroad, "the only roads which could procure prompt protection and immunity from interference [during the Great Strike] were those whose misfortune had made them bankrupt and place them in direct custody and receivers appointed by the United States courts." "To the aid of these roads the United States Marshal could call United States troops," explained Scott, "and no rioter dared to resist the power represented by the small but admirably disciplined detachments quartered near the scenes of the recent troubles."[20]

As time passed, the labor injunction was developed to extend the advantages enjoyed by trains in receivership to solvent roads, other parts of the economy, and to repress different types of labor activity. In 1886, strikes broke out on the Lake Shore and Michigan Southern. Upon request from Lake Shore attorneys, injunctions were issued by state and United States courts. These first injunctions were similar to the "writs of assistance" used during the Great Strike.[21] They allowed for the arrest of any striker interfering with the railroad's right to do business, and

DOI: 10.1057/9781137388117.0005

offenders could be punished for contempt of court without the trouble of a trial by jury. However, there were some differences between these first injunctions and their predecessor. On the one hand, the first injunctions still followed the traditional principle of specifically naming the individuals to be enjoined and directly serving them notice of the enjoinment—a much more restricted and cumbersome process than with the "writs" issued during the Great Strike of 1877. On the other hand, the injunction opened up a much broader possibility of usage. "Writs of assistance" were only applicable to strikes occurring on property in receivership. Although injunctions were traditionally considered "an extraordinary remedy to be invoked only in an emergency characterized by immediate irreparable damage to physical property," they could be used, if the courts allowed, to protect any kind of property, bankrupt or solvent, even if not physically threatened. In order to expand the potential of the injunction, judges had to develop a much broader idea of property—one that included the abstract right to do business. As we have seen, this development was already taking place in other juridical spheres. The injunctions used during the Lake Shore and Michigan Southern strike represent one of the first usages of this more liberal definition of property as defined in *Jacobs*.

The developments in 1886 were not without a tinge of irony. The issuer of the injunction from the United State court, Judge Gresham, based his authority to enjoin striking railway workers on the Enforcement Act—a Reconstruction statue created to protect African Americans from the Ku Klux Klan. This very same law had been emasculated by the Supreme Court in 1876, under the guise of states' rights, giving a "green light to acts of terror [against African Americans] where local officials either could not or would not enforce the law." Indeed, this decision was a key part in the re-enslavement of African Americans in the decades after the Civil War. Now, Judge Gresham was reviving it to empower the federal court to protect the railroads.[22]

As time passed, the injunction continued to evolve. In 1894, Pullman railroad workers went on strike due to a reduction in wages without a similar reduction in rents in the company owned town of Pullman, Illinois. To support the Pullman workers, the American Railway Union (ARU) called for all members to boycott Pullman cars. Upon request by the US District Attorneys, Judge Woods and Judge Grosscup issued an injunction against the ARU and its members for boycotting Pullman cars. The *New York Times* described their injunction as "A Gatling gun

DOI: 10.1057/9781137388117.0005

on paper ... a veritable dragnet ... one of those peculiar instruments that punishes an individual for doing a certain thing, and is equally merciless if he does not do it." The injunction was based on the Sherman Anti-Trust Act of 1890—ostensibly created to curtail the unrelenting concentration of industry and the increase in income and wealth inequality. This hypocrisy was not a surprise to some. The Sherman Anti-Trust Act, explained Senator Orville Platt shortly after its passage, was just the realization of a desire "to get some bill headed: 'A Bill to Punish Trusts' with which to go to the country."[23]

During earlier uses, judges had issued injunctions against multiple railroads and their employees. However, this precedent was greatly expanded during the Pullman strike. Judge Woods and Judge Grosscup issued their injunction against workers on 22 Chicago railroads and served this vast body of workers by means of publications. The *New York Times* explained that "Under this interpretation thousands of strikers might be arrested day after day and be arraigned and summarily dealt with for contempt of court, and this is precisely the policy, according to the reports at the Government Building to-night." The effect was great. "[T]he strike was broken up ... not by the army," explained Eugen Debs, president of URW, "but simply and solely by the action of the United States Courts." Others agreed with Debs' conclusion of the effectiveness of the injunction. "The rapid fire injunction is a great improvement on the gatling gun," explained George Perkins, the president of the Cigar Makers International Union. "Nothing can get beyond its range and it never misses fire."[24]

The application of "writs of assistance" in the 1870s and 1880s and then the first labor injunctions in railroad disputes in the second half of the 1880s and early 1890s followed earlier precedents of government involvement in railroads. The lines had always been quasi-public in nature. Indeed, in the case of "writs of assistance," failed roads were in the explicit care of the court. Thus, it made sense that the courts got involved. At the same time, the path which became increasingly entrenched, especially in the 1890s, was by no means the logical conclusion of government and railroads' close relationship. On the eve of the Pullman Strike, there were still a number of judicial precedents, although a minority, which dealt with railroad strikes in ways more advantageous to labor.[25] However, the Pullman Strike solidified the trend of using courts of equity to defend the rights of employers against the collective strategies of labor. And, in 1895, the Supreme Court, the highest court in the United States, gave its

DOI: 10.1057/9781137388117.0005

official stamp on Judge Woods and Judge Grosscup's decision in *Debs v. United States*—asserting that secondary boycotts in the restraint of trade could be enjoined under the Sherman Anti-Trust Act. Ironically, in the same year, the Supreme Court decided in *United States v. E.C. Knight Co.* that a manufacturing company, even if it controlled 90 percent of sugar refining as did the defendant of the case in question, was excluded from the Sherman Anti-Trust Act because the statute was written to pertain to commerce monopolies—not manufacturing.[26]

With the injunction closing off more and more collective strategies, labor had to find other ways to press its cause. In the last decade of the nineteenth century and the beginning of the twentieth, labor looked to put pressure on unfriendly employers through dissemination of "Don't Patronize" lists. This strategy was incredibly successful for a time.[27] However, in the beginning of the twentieth century the injunction was used to eliminate it. In 1902, the American Federation of Labor (AFL) placed a Connecticut hat manufacturer on the "Don't Patronize" list due to its destruction of the hatters union through firing of union workers and hiring of non-union men. Suffering from a lack of sales, the owner sought refuge in the courts. In 1908, the Supreme Court, in *Loewe v. Lawlor*, decided on the case. It upheld a previous injunction against the boycott awarded by a lesser court and awarded the owner three times the assessed value of abstract damages resulting from the boycott which he claimed amounted to $240,000; members of the hatter's union were ordered to pay.[28] The court based its decision of both the illegality of the boycott and the award of treble damages on the Sherman Anti-Trust Act. In 1911, the Supreme Court, in *Gompers v. Bucks Stove & Range Co.*, ruled once more on the legality of using injunctions to thwart unions from publishing lists of "unfair" companies. As a result of these two discussions, this once successful practice gradually disappeared.[29]

Another development which received the support of the courts was the legality of yellow dog contracts.[30] A yellow dog contract is a signed agreement by an employee stating that he will not join a union. These contracts were almost always signed from a position of vulnerability and gave the employer power over the employee by abridging his basic constitutional rights. From the 1880s until the early 1930s, almost every state law that outlawed yellow dog contracts was struck down.[31] In 1908, the Supreme Court, in *Adair v. United States*, gave its official endorsement of the trend holding that federal and state legislation prohibiting yellow

DOI: 10.1057/9781137388117.0005

dog contracts were unconstitutional because these laws restrained individuals' personal liberty and property.[32]

In 1917, the Supreme Court, in *Hitchman Coal & Coke Co. v. Mitchell*, approved Judge Dayton's injunction against United Mine Workers' (UMW) efforts to unionize miners at the Hitchman Coal and Coke Company. Judge Dayton prohibited UMW from using "argument, reason and persuasion" with Hitchman workers and even forbade the union from "talking to" the miners. This incredible abridgment of basic rights was based on the specious grounds that workers at Hitchman had signed yellow dog contracts, and thus even the peaceful efforts of the UMW constituted "conspiracy to induce breach of contract." Employers reacted enthusiastically to the Supreme Court's decision. By the end of the 1920s, companies had cajoled an estimated 1.25 million workers into signing yellow dog contracts, and injunctions were used more than 60 times during this process to uphold the sanctity of such contracts.[33]

As time passed, the injunction was developed to cover more and more aspects of employer–employee relations. Indeed, by the 1920s, judges had so skilfully adjudicated laws and transformed the idea of property as to stretch the injunction to apply to unionizing workers who had signed anti-union contracts, secondary boycotts, picketing, the calling of strikes by union leaders, unionizing of nonunionized sectors of the economy, and the printing of lists of businesses thought to be unfair toward labor. In the mid-1890s after the Supreme Court gave its official approval to the use of injunctions against secondary boycotts, Governor Altgeld of Illinois contended that "Under this new order of things a federal judge becomes at once a legislator, court and executioner." "A federal judge could now issue an order at the behest of some corporation attorney," explained Altgeld, "prohibiting most anything, including that which the law did not forbid. Thus could the judge legislate and, having done so, proceed to arrest people and, without a trial, to imprison them, not for disobeying any statue but on the pretext that they had violated his injunction."[34] Curiously, the system that became more and more entrenched as time passed was very similar to that proposed by Tom Scott, President of the Pennsylvania Railroad, after the Great Strike of 1877. From that early period, Scott was already arguing to extend the power embodied in the "writs of assistance" to protect all trains. "The laws which give the Federal courts the summary process of injunction to restrain so comparatively trifling a wrong as an infringement of a patent-right," implored Scott, "certainly it must have been intended or ought to give the United States authority to prevent a wrong-doing which not only destroys a particular road, but also paralyzes the entire commerce of the country and wastes the national wealth."[35]

General trend

As time passed, rule by injunction became ever more entrenched. The application of the labor injunction became both increasingly effective and was applied more and more to regulate labor affairs. In Figure 3.3, I present data on the percentage of all strikes and secondary strikes enjoined per decade from the 1870s through the 1920s.[36] These trends provide a good first approximation of the de facto orientation of laws and institutions throughout this period. As we can see, the usage of the injunction in all strikes and secondary strikes became increasingly common throughout the final decades of the nineteenth century and into the first decade of the twentieth century.

In the 1880s, at least 1 percent of all strikes and 10 percent of secondary strikes were enjoined. In the 1890s, the percentage of all strikes and secondary strikes enjoined reached 3 and 15 percent respectively. The usage of injunctions against secondary boycotts accelerated in the 1900s during which period at least 29 percent of secondary strikes were enjoined. However, the percentage of all strikes enjoined stayed the same from the previous decade. This might be a result of the data. The figure for this decade only covers 1900 through 1905. It could be that

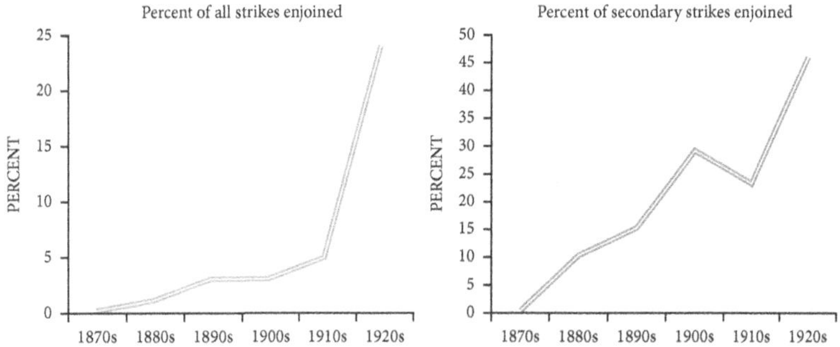

FIGURE 3.3 *The orientation of laws and institutions from the 1870s through the 1920s*

Source: Forbath (1991).

DOI: 10.1057/9781137388117.0005

in the second half of this decade a larger percentage of all strikes were enjoined.

The successive slanting of laws and institutions to favor business was not missed by contemporaries. During the 1912 presidential campaign, Woodrow Wilson insisted that the federal government be utilized to restore market competition and local self-governance "by strengthening anti-trust laws, protecting the right of workers to unionize, and actively encouraging small entrepreneurs." For Wilson and many others, the late nineteenth century was not a time of free competition but of government subservience to big business.[37] The growth of the injunction as a means of regulating labor and the state and federal governments' growing role in enforcing injunctions was the major driver of that trend.

During the Progressive Era, which lasted from the 1900s to the end of Wilson's presidency in 1920, laws and institutions were reoriented to arch toward equality. Indeed, we can see from Figure 3.3 that the application of injunctions to secondary strikes decreased in the second decade of the twentieth century. However, the Progressive Era was much more than just a reduction in the usage of the injunction. From 1900 to World War I, the Progressives pushed through Congress a number of liberal laws. For example, in 1906, explains historian Richard Hofstadter, the Hepburn Act became law—representing the first sincere effort to regulate the railroads. Also, the current income tax was a product of the Progressive movement. Through the passage of the Sixteenth Amendment and the Revenue Act of 1913, the income tax was successfully reestablished over the Supreme Court's 1895 decision against its constitutionality.[38] The surtax rates and the amount of income subject to surtaxes were increased multiple times throughout the remainder of the Progressive Era.[39]

At the same time, many of the laws passed by the Progressives either did not attempt to reverse the orientation of previous laws or, if they did, they met the same fate as their nineteenth-century predecessors. For example, the Clayton Act and the Federal Trade Commission (FTC) did not conflict with any of the Supreme Court's detrimental decisions on the Interstate Commerce Act and the Sherman Anti-Trust Act. Furthermore, President Woodrow Wilson both understaffed the FTC and appointed people that were unsympathetic to reform. Indeed, Louis Brandeis who helped to create the FTC later described its management under President Wilson as "a stupid administration." Also, some legislative gains during

DOI: 10.1057/9781137388117.0005

this period met the same fate as the Sherman Anti-Trust Act. For example, the Child Labor Act of 1916 prohibited the interstate sale of goods which were produced by laborers under the age of 14. However, only two years after it became law, in *Hammer v. Dagenhart*, the Supreme Court declared it unconstitutional, "on the grounds that Congress could not use its commerce powers to regulate labor conditions."[40]

During the 1920s, Progressive impulses floundered and government was taken over by those with big business's interests at heart. The American businessman is "the most influential person in the nation," exclaimed the organ of the Chamber of Commerce, *Nation's Business*, in 1925. It now occupies "a position of leadership which the businessman has never held before." We can see part of this reversal in the aggressive increase in usage of the injunction against all strikes and secondary strikes depicted in Figure 3.3. Indeed, in the 1920s, the court enjoined at least 25 percent of all strikes and 46 percent of secondary strikes. We also saw this trend in the string of Supreme Court's decisions (*Coronado Coal Co. v. United Mine, Workers, American Steel Foundries v. Tri-city Central Trades Council, Truax v. Corrigan*) detrimental to labor. At the same time, the reversals of the 1920s spilled into other spheres.

For example, the Revenue Act of 1921 reduced the maximum surtax to 50 percent and the amount of income subject to it. In addition, the act repealed the excess-profits tax which had been a large source of government revenue during the war and the focus of much of business's odium. The Revenue Act of 1924 reduced the maximum surtax to 40 percent and again reduced the amount of income subject to the surtax. And the Revenue Act of 1926 cut the maximum surtax of 1924 in half leaving it at 20 percent of incomes over $14,000. These dramatic decreases in the maximum surtax rate were not counter-balanced with equal decreases in tax rates for lower income groups. Indeed, the gains from changes in tax laws during the 1920s went almost exclusively to those at the upper reaches of the income ladder. For example, between 1923 and 1929, an individual earning the equivalent of $63,000 in 2014 dollars before taxes would have seen his disposable yearly income increased by 1 percent after the multiple reductions in taxes during the 1920s. On the other hand, an individual earning the equivalent of $12.6 million in 2014 dollars before taxes would have seen his disposable yearly income increased by 31 percent as a result of the reductions in surtax rates and the amount of income subject to the different surtaxes.[41]

Conclusion

To get an idea of the relationship between the evolution of de facto laws and institutions and income inequality, in Figure 3.4, I graph the percentage of all strikes and secondary strikes that were enjoined by decade against the average income share of the top 1 percent.[42] As we can see, there is a strong positive relationship between income inequality and the orientation of laws and institutions. Decades where the labor injunction was more vigorously enforced against all strikes and secondary strikes are coincident with a higher average income share for the top 1 percent of tax units. Decades where the labor injunction was less vigorously enforced against all strikes and secondary strikes are coincident with a lower average income share for the top 1 percent of tax units.

In terms of the theory looked at in the last chapter, in the 1870s and early 1880s, workers' collective activities more effectively counterbalanced employers' wage setting powers. Outcomes were closer to the perfect world where workers are paid a wage equal to their marginal product. Beginning in the mid-1880s, the labor injunction was used to redraw employer–employee relations. Workers' collective activities were stymied more and more, and employers' wage setting power became increasingly unchecked. As a result, the difference between the wage and marginal product for the average worker increased. The resulting increase in profits and the reduction in labor's voice in the firm and society reduced opposition to increasing remuneration for those at the top and income inequality increased.

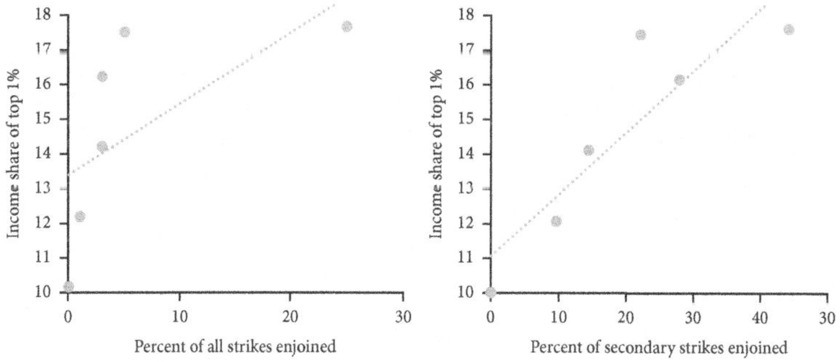

FIGURE 3.4 *Coincidence of change in laws and institutions and income inequality*
Source: Author.

DOI: 10.1057/9781137388117.0005

Thus, the period spanning from the Gilded Age through the New Era in the United States was remarkably similar to the present. During both periods, laws and institutions were oriented to embrace inequality by empowering minority groups in the economic realm at the expense of the majority and balancing taxation on regressive sources. At the same time, the income share of the top 1 percent was rising, and, at the end of both of these periods or the farthest point reached during the current period, the income share of the top 1 percent reached a high in US history. The laws of the Gilded Age and the New Era were definitely more repressive. This might have been a result of the relatively smaller size of the economic pie at the time. However, the regressive nature of laws and institutions today should not be downplayed. Interestingly, nondemocratic elements of our political system were central during both periods. In the nineteenth and early twentieth centuries, the judicial branch was crucial in developing the labor injunction, extending its reach, and increasing its usage. Over the last three and a half decades, the quasi-judicial NLRB played a central role in reorienting employer–employee relations. How has all this been possible? How have such unequal outcomes persisted and intensified for such long periods in US history? To these questions, we now turn.

Notes

1 Data for the nineteenth century is taken from Thomas Piketty and Emmanuel Saez's series. The red line excludes capital gains and the blue line includes capital gains. What looks like a small check mark on the left edge of the graph is the statistics for the income share of the top 1 percent of tax units in 1866, 1867, and 1868 calculated in Stelzner, M. (2014a). "Income Inequality in the United States in the Late 1860s," working paper. This series includes capital gains on assets that were held for less than three years.

2 See Fairman, C. (July 01, 1953). "The So-Called Granger Cases, Lord Hale, and Justice Bradley," *Stanford Law Review*, 5(4), pp. 587–679.

3 Massachusetts pioneered this trend forming a labor bureau in 1869.

4 See Fishback, P. V., Holmes, R., & Allen, S. (January 01, 2009). "Lifting the Curse of Dimensionality: Measures of the States' Labor Legislation Climate in the United States during the Progressive Era," *Labor History*, 50(3).

5 See Fairman, C. (July 01, 1953). "The So-Called Granger Cases, Lord Hale, and Justice Bradley," *Stanford Law Review*, 5(4), pp. 587–679.

6 Montgomery, D. (1987). *The Fall of the House of Labor: The Workplace, the State, and American Labor Activism, 1865–1925*. Cambridgeshire: Cambridge University Press. p. 165.

DOI: 10.1057/9781137388117.0005

7 See Fairman, C. (July 01, 1953). "The So-Called Granger Cases, Lord Hale, and Justice Bradley," *Stanford Law Review*, 5(4), pp. 587–679.

8 See David, H. (1958). *The History of the Haymarket Affair: A Study in the American Social-Revolutionary and Labor Movements*. New York: Russell & Russell. pp. 30–6.

9 Redemption refers to the period where Southern Democrats retook control of state governments after Reconstruction.

10 See Foner, E. (1988). *Reconstruction: America's Unfinished Revolution, 1863–1877*. New York: Harper & Row. pp. 593–6. Also see Woodward, C. V. (1951). *Origins of the New South, 1877–1913*. Baton Rouge: Louisiana State University Press. And Blackmon, D. A. (2008). *Slavery by Another Name: The Re-Enslavement of Black Americans from the Civil War to World War II*. New York: Doubleday.

11 See 98 NY at 115.

12 See 98 NY 98 (1885).

13 Fine, S. (1956). *Laissez Faire and the General-Welfare State: A Study of Conflict in American Thought, 1865–1901*. Ann Arbor: University of Michigan Press. p. 141.

14 See Forbath, W. E. (1991). *Law and the Shaping of the American Labor Movement*. Cambridge, MA: Harvard University Press. pp. 37–9, Appendix A. Also, see Paul, A. M. (1960). *Conservative Crisis and the Rule of Law: Attitudes of Bar and Bench, 1887–1895*. Ithaca, NY: Published for the American Historical Association [by] Cornell University Press.

15 Index was calculated by author using data from Forbath (1991). I leave out the twentieth century because at that point Forbath's data are no longer comprehensive. See Forbath, W. E. (1991). *Law and the Shaping of the American Labor Movement*. Cambridge, MA: Harvard University Press. pp. 37–9, Appendix A.

16 See Forbath, W. E. (1991). *Law and the Shaping of the American Labor Movement*. Cambridge, MA: Harvard University Press.

17 See Bruce, R. V. (1959). *1877: Year of Violence*. Indianapolis: Bobbs-Merrill.

18 Learning from the successful strategy employed by the Reading Railroad in an earlier strike, trunk lines agreed to pooling arrangement for westbound traffic. There is evidence they had secret agreements for eastbound traffic. These arrangements insured members of their share of revenue in the case of a strike. As a result, roads could one by one reduce wages without the risk associated with the same strategy if carried out individually. See Bruce, R. V. (1959). *1877: Year of Violence*. Indianapolis: Bobbs-Merrill. pp. 41–2.

19 Judge Gresham of Indianapolis participated indirectly in the issuance of "writs of assistance." During the strike, he helped organize a vigilance committee and thus excused himself from directly ruling on cases pertaining to the strike. However, he asked his good friend Judge Drummond to take

DOI: 10.1057/9781137388117.0005

his place, and sat beside him on the bench whispering in his ear when necessary. See Friedman, G. (1998). *State-Making and Labor Movements: France and the United States, 1876–1914*. Ithaca: Cornell University Press. p. 175; Bruce, R. V. (1959). *1877: Year of Violence*. Indianapolis: Bobbs-Merrill. pp. 308–9.

20 Some strikes did resist, and as a result a number of arrests and convictions took place. As the labor historian William Forbath explains, "[T]heir convictions marked a signal turning point in the history of equity practice. They were the first contempt sanctions exercised against persons neither parties nor named by court orders." See Forbath, W. E. (1991). *Law and the Shaping of the American Labor Movement*. Cambridge, MA: Harvard University Press. p. 67. For Thomas Scott quote, see Scott, T. A. (September 01, 1877). "The Recent Strikes." *The North American Review*, 125(258), pp. 351–62.

21 Some injunctions were also issued during the Great Southwest Strike of the same year. "Writs of assistance" were also prominent. See McMurry, Donald L. (1961). "The Legal Ancestry of the Pullman Strike Injunctions," *Industrial and Labor Relations Review*, 14(2) (January 1961), pp. 235–56. And Forbath, W. E. (1991). *Law and the Shaping of the American Labor Movement*. Cambridge, MA: Harvard University Press.

22 For the Lake Shore Strikes, see McMurry, Donald L. (1961). "The Legal Ancestry of the Pullman Strike Injunctions," *Industrial and Labor Relations Review*, 14(2) (January 1961), pp. 235–56. For the 1876 Supreme Court decision, see Foner, E. (1988). *Reconstruction: America's unfinished revolution, 1863–1877*. New York: Harper & Row. p. 531. For more on the re-enslavement of African Americans after the Civil War, see Blackmon, D. A. (2008). *Slavery by another name: The re-enslavement of Black Americans from the Civil War to World War II*. New York: Doubleday.

23 See Lindsey, A. (1964). *The Pullman Strike: The Story of a Unique Experiment and of a Great Labor Upheaval*. Chicago: University of Chicago Press; McMurry, Donald L. (1961). "The Legal Ancestry of the Pullman Strike Injunctions," *Industrial and Labor Relations Review*,14(2) (January 1961), pp. 235–56; and David, H. (1958) *The History of the Haymarket Affair: A Study in the American Social-Revolutionary and Labor Movements*. New York: Russell & Russell.; and Goldstein, R. J. (1978). *Political Repression in Modern America from 1870 to the Present*. Boston: G. K. Hall. p. 59. The *New York Times*, "Cars Must Not Be Stopped," July 3, 1894, p. 1. These developments omit more positive and negative decisions. For example, in 1893, Judge Jenkins held strikes in general to be enjoinable because their nature was always evil. However, the cases explained earlier represent the general trend. For Senator Platt's comment, see Hofstadter, R. (1955). *The Age of Reform: From Bryan to F.D.R.* New York: Knopf. pp. 243–4.

24 Quoted from Friedman, G. (1998). *State-Making and Labor Movements: France and the United States, 1876–1914*. Ithaca: Cornell University Press. p. 180 footnote 93.

DOI: 10.1057/9781137388117.0005

25 Forbath, W. E. (1991). *Law and the Shaping of the American Labor Movement.* Cambridge, MA: Harvard University Press. pp. 80–1.

26 See Friedman, G. (1999). *State-Making and Labor Movements: France and the United States, 1876–1914*. p. 176; Lindsey, A. (1964). *The Pullman Strike: The Story of a Unique Experiment and of a Great Labor Upheaval.* Chicago: University of Chicago Press; McMurry, Donald L. (1961). "The Legal Ancestry of the Pullman Strike Injunctions," *Industrial and Labor Relations Review*, 14(2) (January 1961), pp. 235–56; and David, H. (1958) *The History of the Haymarket Affair: A Study in the American Social-Revolutionary and Labor Movements.* New York: Russell & Russell.; and Goldstein, R. J. (1978). *Political Repression in Modern America from 1870 to the present.* Boston: G.K. Hall. p. 59.

27 See Forbath, W. E. (1991). *Law and the Shaping of the American Labor Movement.* Cambridge, MA: Harvard University Press. pp. 90–1.

28 The manufacturer–plaintiff lawyer, Walter Merritt, was able to obtain information on which of the union members had homes or bank accounts from which the enormous sum could be paid. See Lawlor v. Loewe, 235 U.S. 522, 536–37 (1915), pp. 202–3.

29 See Forbath, W. E. (1991). *Law and the Shaping of the American Labor Movement.* Cambridge, MA: Harvard University Press. p. 94.

30 In the 1870s and 1880s, yellow dog contracts were called "iron clad" contracts.

31 See Forbath, W. E. (1991). *Law and the Shaping of the American Labor Movement.* Cambridge, MA: Harvard University Press. p. 114 footnote 65.

32 See Leuchtenburg, W. E. (1958). *The Perils of Prosperity, 1914–32*. Chicago: University of Chicago Press. pp. 199–200; and Bernstein, I. (1960). *The lean years: A history of the American worker, 1920–1933*. Boston: Houghton Mifflin.

33 For Supreme Court decisions, see Roche, J. P. (January 01, 1963). "Entrepreneurial Liberty and the Fourteenth Amendment." *Labor History*, 4(1), pp. 3–31; and Bernstein, I. (1960). *The Lean Years: A History of the American Worker, 1920–1933*. Boston: Houghton Mifflin. For application of the injunction, see Witte, E. E. (1969). *The Government in Labor Disputes*. New York: Arno. For Judge Jenkin's decision, see McMurry, Donald L. (1961). "The Legal Ancestry of the Pullman Strike Injunctions," *Industrial and Labor Relations Review*, 14(2) (January 1961), pp. 235–56.

34 For Altgeld quote, see Lindsey, A. (1964). *The Pullman Strike: The Story of a Unique Experiment and of a Great Labor Upheaval.* Chicago: University of Chicago Press. p. 299.

35 Scott, T. A. (September 01, 1877). "The Recent Strikes." *The North American Review*,125(258), pp. 351–62.

36 Data come from Forbath. Ibid. (See appendix B). In terms of secondary strikes, only injunctions used against such activities are considered in the statistic.

DOI: 10.1057/9781137388117.0005

37 Foner, E. (1998). *The Story of American Freedom*. New York: W.W. Norton. pp. 121–2.

38 On the 1895 Supreme Court decision, see Goldstein, R. J. (1978). *Political Repression in Modern America from 1870 to the Present*. Boston: G. K. Hall. p. 59.

39 The Revenue Act of 1916 increased the maximum surtax from 6 to 13 percent and slightly increased the amount of income subject to the highest surtax. The Revenue Act of October 3, 1917 dramatically increased both the maximum surtax rate and the amount of income subject to the highest surtax such that all incomes above $7,500 were subject to a surtax of 63 percent. The Revenue Act of 1918, which was passed in February 1919, increased the maximum surtax by 2 more percentage points pushing the rate to its highest point in the period. For specifics on income tax, see *Report of the Secretary of the Treasury*, 1940, pp. 466–79 & 530–3. For specifics on tariff, see Ratner, S. (1980). *Taxation and Democracy in America*. New York: Octagon Books. pp. 323–4.

40 On inheritance tax, see Ratner, S. (1980). *Taxation and Democracy in America*. New York: Octagon Books. pp. 234–7, 243–4, 247–9. On Hepburn Act, see Hofstadter, R. (1955). *The Age of Reform: From Bryan to F.D.R.* New York: Knopf. p. 252. For Federal Trade Commission and Clayton Act, see Hofstadter ibid. pp. 249–50. For Court decisions, see Leuchtenburg, W. E. (1958). *The Perils of Prosperity, 1914–32*. Chicago: University of Chicago Press. Pp. 99–100.

41 Although these legislated changes in tax were large, they were not the whole story. The Secretary of Treasurer from 1920 to 1932 and one of the richest men in the United States, Andrew Mellow, was found to have dispensed large refunds, credits, and abatements to those in the upper reaches of the income ladder. What taxes Treasurer Mellon "could not reduce [through legislation], he could often refund—a process which had the advantage of taking place behind closed doors," explains historian Arthur Schlesinger in his book on the 1920s. "In the first eight years at the Treasury, the Secretary dispensed $3.5 billion in the shape of cash refunds, credits, and abatements. The size of these disbursements mounted steadily during the period, except in 1927 and 1930, when congressional grumbling forced the Treasury to hold back." On change in taxation, see *Report of the Secretary of the Treasury*, 1940, pp. 466–79 & 530–3; Soule, G. H. (1947). *Prosperity Decade: From War to Depression: 1917–1929*. New York: Rinehart. pp. 317–18; and Leuchtenburg, W. E. (1958). *The Perils of Prosperity, 1914–32*. Chicago: University of Chicago Press. P. 98. On Mellon, see Schlesinger, A. M. (1957). *The Age of Roosevelt*. Boston: Houghton Mifflin. pp. 62–3.

42 Income share data are from the sources used in Figure 3.1. I create decade averages based on the average trend and using data from the current income tax when applicable.

DOI: 10.1057/9781137388117.0005

4
Mixed Results

Abstract: *In Chapter 4, I examine the general trend in the orientation of laws and institutions and income inequality in the United States from the mid-1930s through the 1970s. I show that laws were made more inclusive and the income share of the top 1 percent decreased. I then explore some explanations for why we have such a mixed record of ameliorating income inequality in the United States when our political system is based on equality. Finding these explanations lacking, the chapter ends in suspense.*

Stelzner, Mark. *Economic Inequality and Policy Control in the United States*. New York: Palgrave Macmillan, 2015.
DOI: 10.1057/9781137388117.0006.

Let us finally address the question that has been lingering in the background: in a democracy where substantial income inequality exists and it is not solely the result of differential productivity, why doesn't the poor majority implement laws to counter the spheres of power in the economic realm or institute a significant and constant level of redistribution? As we have seen in the first three chapters, there are long periods where laws and institutions are made more and more exclusive. With the exception of the Progressive Era, laws and institutions were oriented more and more to benefit narrow groups from the end of Reconstruction to the outbreak of the Great Depression. During this period, the income share of the top 1 percent went from somewhere between 9 and 10 percent of all income in the late 1860s to 19.3 percent in 1916 and 23.94 percent in 1928. Likewise, we saw in Chapter 2 that laws and institutions have been made increasingly more exclusive since the 1980s, and the income share of the top 1 percent has increased from somewhere between 8 and 10 percent of all income in the late 1970s to 22.46 percent in 2012.

To be sure, there are periods when our political system seems to work for the benefit of the majority. For example, beginning in the mid-1930s and accelerating during World War II, laws and institutions were reconfigured to stem the growth of and even reduce income inequality. For example, the National Labor Relations Act (NLRA) was signed into law in 1935. As we have seen in Chapter 3, workers' rights to bargain collectively were abrogated more and more from the beginning of Redemption through the end of the New Era. Empowered under the NLRA and NLRB, union membership as a percentage of total employment increased dramatically in the United States starting at less than 8 percent in the beginning of the 1930s and reaching 19.2 percent by the end of the decade. Union membership continued to increase in the 1940s reaching 27.1 percent by the mid-decade. After which, it fell throughout the remaining years of the 1940s but began increasing again in 1951. And, in 1954, union membership as a percentage of total employment reached 28.2 percent—the highest value in US history.

As shown in Chapter 2, these increases in union membership would have had the effect of countering employers' wage setting powers and thus bringing the wage closer and closer to the marginal product. Profits would have decreased reducing room for absorbent CEO pay. At the same time, increased union strength would have created formidable opposition to high CEO remuneration. Thus, the income share of the top 1 percent would likely have decreased.

DOI: 10.1057/9781137388117.0006

The Fair Labor Standards Act (FLSA), which created a minimum wage, a maximum workweek, and abolished child labor, was signed into law in 1938. The monumental change this law represented can be seen by the fact that just two decades earlier the Supreme Court had ruled that laws which regulated child labor, and the labor market in general, were unconstitutional.[1] From the passage of the FLSA through the 1970s, the nominal value of the minimum wage was increased a number of times. In Figure 4.1, I display data on the real minimum wage in the years that the nominal value was changed. As we can see, nominal increases from the late 1930s through the 1960s represented real increases in the value of the minimum wage. In 1968, the real value of the minimum wage reached a peak at $10.69 in 2013 money. After which, changes in the nominal value of the minimum wage in the 1970s held its purchasing power constant at around nine and a half dollars. In the 1980s and thereafter, the minimum wage suffered a fate similar to that of the NLRA—its real value was allowed to deteriorate as the price level increased over time.[2]

Like the change in laws and institution to support unionization, increases in the minimum wage would have also countered employers' monopsony power forcing firms to pay a wage closer to the marginal product. As the real value of the wage was increased between the late 1930s through the 1960s, the difference between the wage and what

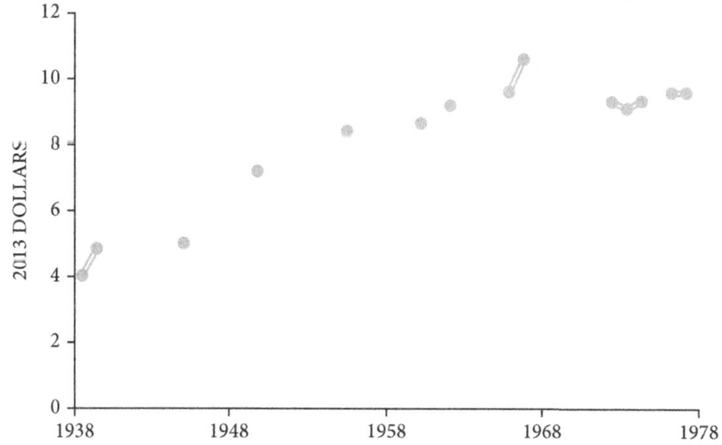

FIGURE 4.1 *Real federal minimum wage in the United States*

Source: US Department of Labor: http://www.dol.gov/whd/minwage/chart.htm

workers added to production at the margin would have decreased. As a result, profits would have decreased leaving less room for absorbent CEO remuneration.

Another monumental act passed during this period was the Servicemen's Readjustment Act of 1944, more commonly known as the GI Bill. The GI Bill offered soldiers that had served at least three months of active duty and had not received a dishonorable discharge access to loans for starting a business, to buy a house, funding for college or vocational training, and job placement services. The bill "gave generations of veterans a chance…to build strong families and good lives, and [a chance] to change the face of America," explained President Bill Clinton in a speech honoring the bill's fiftieth anniversary. These statements were not mere platitudes. Government put vast amounts of money behind the bill. By the late 1940s, GI Bill spending accounted for 15 percent of the federal budget. From the year it was enacted to 1971, federal spending under the GI Bill surpassed $95 billion. Over a fifth of a million used credit provided by the bill to buy farms and start businesses. More than 5 million GIs utilized house mortgages which capped interest rates and reduced requirements for down payments. By mid-1950, over two million GIs had attained higher education under the bill, and almost 6 million had used funding from the bill to attend vocational training programs. For most veterans, the GI Bill paid full tuition and a stipend for living expenses. Under the schooling opportunities offered by the bill, the federal government spent more by 1950 than the entire expenditures on the Marshall Plan, "which had successfully rebuilt Europe's devastated economic life after the war."[3]

Because the vast majority of soldiers didn't come from the top 1 percent or even the top 10 percent of the population and because the income tax during this period was much more progressive, the GI Bill represented a significant transfer between income groups playing a leading role in growing the middle class in the United States after World War II.[4] Indeed, the bill, contended President Clinton in concluding his speech in its memory, was "the best deal ever made by Uncle Sam, [it was a moment] when dreams came true."[5]

The NLRA, the FLSA, and the GI Bill are just a few of many changes initiated in the 1930s which were extended to some degree or another through the 1960s. These changes represented a dramatic shift in the orientation of laws and institutions in the United States. As a result, the income share of the top 1 percent fell precipitously from around

DOI: 10.1057/9781137388117.0006

24 percent in the late 1920s to between 11 and 13 percent by the end of the 1940s. By the early 1960s, it had dropped to around 10 percent of all income. Income inequality continued to fall from the mid-1960s through the 1970s. And by the late 1970s, the income share of the top 1 percent was around 9 percent of all income. However, the fall in the income share of the top 1 percent during this later period could not have been due to change in the minimum wage, laws protecting unionization, or the GI Bill. As we can see from Figure 4.1, the real minimum wage reached its peak in 1968 and then fell but was maintained at relatively high plateau throughout the 1970s. Laws and institutions empowering unions and unionization reached a peak earlier on and maintained a series of descending plateaus until things changed dramatically, to the detriment of unions in the 1980s.

Instead, change during the end of this period occurred in two new directions: increased civil and political rights for African Americans which brought with it increased economic freedom, and, increased environmental protection which forced business to internalize externalities. Let's look at Civil Rights first. A central, yet often unrecognized, factor of the New Deal and Fair Deal legislation, explains historian Ira Katznelson in his book, *When Affirmative Action Was White*, was that it was systematically designed to protect Jim Crow laws and thus excluded African Americans in the South.[6] Southern House Representatives and Senators made up a key voting block for the passage of all Democratic legislation during the New and Fair Deal. The South was keen on extending aid to its region which represented the poorest area in the United States throughout this period. However, for southern politicians, such welfare gains were second to protecting the peculiar nature of their economic and political institutions. As a result, northern Democrats had to oblige their southern bedfellows. "Franklin Roosevelt has been hindered," commented W. E. B. Du Bois in the *People's Voice* in 1944, "by the necessity of not going so far as to lose entirely the support of the South."[7] Comments like these were common in the African American press throughout the North. "Northern Negroes who vote a Democratic President in office," remarked the *Pittsburgh Courier* in 1940, "put the South in the saddle. The South runs our Congress, Army and our Navy, and there is not very much left of the country after that."[8]

Southern Congressmen achieved these goals not by explicitly limiting New and Fair Deal legislation to white Americans but by inserting

DOI: 10.1057/9781137388117.0006

provisions that, in Robert Lieberman's words, were "racially laden."[9] They did this in three ways, explains Katznelson. First, the "most important instances concerned categories of work in which blacks were heavily overrepresented, notably farmworkers and maids." Making up more than 75 percent of the African American labor force in the South, farm and domestic workers were excluded from the NLRA, the FLPA, Social Security, and other New Deal and Fair Deal legislation. Second, Southern Congressmen "successfully insisted that the administration of these and other laws, including assistance to the poor and support for veterans," continues Katznelson, "be placed in the hands of local officials who were deeply hostile to black aspirations." Third, Southern politicians prevented "Congress from attaching any sort of anti-discrimination provisions to a wide array of social welfare programs such as community health services, school lunches, and hospital construction grants, indeed all the programs that distributed monies to their region."[10]

As a result, although income inequality decreased significantly from the 1930s through the 1960s in the United States as a whole, African Americans fell further and further behind white Americans. "Between 1949 and 1959, the income of Negro men relative to white men declined in every section of this country," lamented President Lyndon Johnson in a speech at Howard University on June 4, 1965. "We have pursued" justice, continued Johnson, "faithfully to the edge of our imperfections, and we have failed to find it for the American Negro."[11] President Johnson's answer to these injustices was the Civil Rights Act (CRA), which passed Congress nearly a year before the 1965 Howard University speech, the Voting Rights Act (VRA), which would pass Congress that same summer, and affirmative action.

In terms of the affirmative action, change began the next year. In March 1966, the Equal Employment Opportunity Commission which was created by the CRA required all employers and unions under its jurisdiction to submit forms on the racial composition of their workforce and membership, respectively. Affirmative action was later secured under an executive order by President Nixon and the Supreme Court decision, *Griggs v. Duke Power Company* in 1971.[12] "Federal agencies and federal courts," explains Katznelson, "soon required that employers and educators take race into account in order to rectify the second-class status of African Americans." Nixon's executive order went a step further requiring hiring of minority laborers in construction trades in proportion to their percentage of the local labor force. With these changes, the

DOI: 10.1057/9781137388117.0006

burden of proof of discrimination shifted from showing evidence of specific discriminatory acts to justification of outcomes in employment, membership, and enrollment.[13]

By increasing civil and political freedoms and by directly confronting discrimination and putting the burden of proof on employers, the Civil Rights movement increased economic freedom of African Americans. Market friction, and in this case barriers, which confronted African Americans throughout the labor market, diminished significantly. If we want to think about this in terms of the theory laid out in Chapter 2, this would have the effect of flattening the labor supply curve which was most likely much more steeply sloped than that of southern and northern whites. This flatter supply curve would decrease the degree to which employers could reduce the wage below the marginal product—it would reduce employers' monopsony power. As a result, for those firms which capitalized on the second-class nature of African American citizenship before the Civil Rights movement, profits and most likely remuneration for those at the top of those firms would have decreased as a result of the change during the 1960s and 1970s.[14]

In terms of environmental legislation, from "1969 to 1972, virtually the entire American business community," explains political scientist David Vogel in his book, *Fluctuating Fortunes*, "experienced a series of political setbacks without parallel in the postwar period."[15] In December 1969, Congress passed the National Environmental Protection Act (NEPA) which declared "the improvement of the quality of the environment to be a major priority."[16] The aim of NEPA, and the following array of environmental legislation, was to force businesses to internalize some of their externalities. Six months later, the Nixon administration established the Environmental Protection Agency (EPA) in order to administer the new regulation and to take over a number of other state regulatory functions. A year later, Congress passed the 1970 Clean Air Act which was a major change from the 1967 Clean Air Act. It contained firm legislative times for pollution abatement of stationary plants and required car companies to reduce vehicular emissions of hydrocarbons and carbon monoxide by 90 percent by 1976. And, two years later, Congress passed the Federal Water Pollution Control Amendments and the Federal Environmental Pesticide Control Act of 1972.[17]

The legislation flowing out of Congress in the late 1960s and early 1970s dramatically increased government regulation of business. "Between 1970 and 1975," explains Vogel, "expenditures by federal social regulatory agencies increased from $1.5 to $4.3 billion."[18] As mentioned earlier, the aim of that regulation was to force business to internalize costs that it had previously placed on the general public. Between 1970 and 1974, real business spending on air pollution controls increased by over 150 percent. The total spending on air and water pollution in 1974 amounted to 7.7 percent of all capital formation by manufacturing firms. In contrast, in 1969, total spending on air- and water-pollution controls and *occupational safety equipment* only amounted to 4 percent of capital formation.[19]

How do NEPA and other environmental legislation of this period fit into our story? Degrading the environment during the production process forces a cost on the community. At the same time, it creates a benefit for the business that pollutes—a reduction in the cost of production. What essentially is taking place is redistribution from the community to the polluting business. It is like business is receiving a subsidy from the government which is funded through a tax on the community. Although there is the nuance of low-income community members whose jobs *might* depend on a low cost of production, regulation of business's ability to pollute seems to fit with our story. Indeed, the creation of regulations that force business to reduce pollutants is like the reduction or termination of a subsidy for business and the reduction or elimination of the tax on the community to fund it, all at the same time. These developments also likely put pressure on profits and, as a result, remuneration for those at the top.

Concurrent and parallel changes also took place in other realms. Simultaneous with the new environmental regulation, Congress passed, and Nixon signed into law, the Tax Reform Act of 1969. The legislation increased the "maximum tax on capital gains, limited real estate depreciation schedules, eliminated the tax credit for investment, and reduced the depletion allowance for a number of natural substances, including oil and gas. At the same time, it provided a modest amount of tax relief for the middle class and the poor."[20] All and all, the tax reform dramatically shifted the burden of taxation onto business. Indeed, the elimination of the tax credit alone increased the corporate tax burden by almost $3 billion.[21] *The New Republic* exclaimed that the 1969 Tax Reform Act "is far and away the most 'anti-rich' tax reform proposal ever proposed by a Republican President in the 56 years of the existence of the income tax."[22]

DOI: 10.1057/9781137388117.0006

General trend

Although not always in the same form, there seem to be periods when laws and institutions are set up to reduce inequality and the income share of the top 1 percent is decreasing and times where laws and institutions are set up to embrace inequality and the share of the top 1 percent is increasing. To summarize, in Figure 4.2, I display the income share of the top 1 percent from the late 1860s to the present. As we can see, the two periods where laws and institutions were made more exclusive and income inequality was rising are punctuated by a period where laws and institutions were made more inclusive and income inequality was falling.

There are exceptions to the trend in any of the three periods. For example, the Taft Hartley Act of 1947 moved in the opposite direction of New Deal legislation by prohibiting certain union actions. Also, the liberal tendencies during the Progressive Era, especially Woodrow Wilson's two terms as President do not fit well with the overall trend from the 1870s through the 1920s. During this time, the income share of the top 1 percent decreased significantly. However, for now, let us set these exceptions aside and focus on understanding the general trends during the three periods depicted in Figure 4.2 in the context of our political system.[23] Later, we will return to these exceptions.

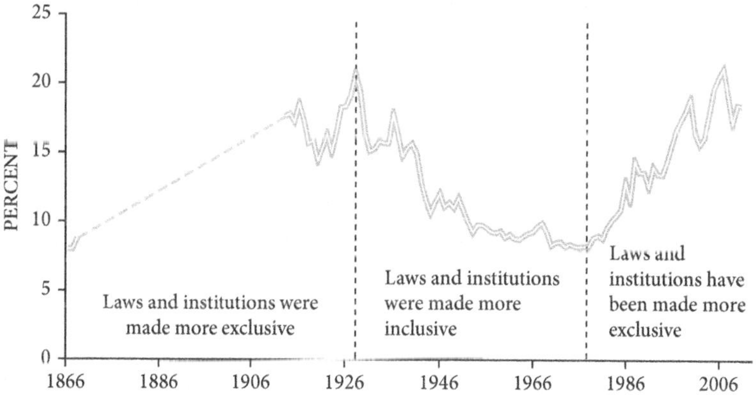

FIGURE 4.2 *Periods in US history—evolution of income inequality and the orientation of laws and institutions*

Source: Author.

DOI: 10.1057/9781137388117.0006

How do we explain the evolution of the orientation of laws and institutions and income inequality in the United States from the 1870s to the present? Why doesn't the poor majority implement laws that counter the spheres of power in the economic realm or maintain a constant level of redistribution in a political system where they are seemingly empowered? Indeed, why are there long periods where the majority seems to be disempowered?

Is our democracy a sham?

Many have questioned the sincerity of our political system. "As a nation, we began by declaring that 'all men are created equal,'"[24] wrote Abraham Lincoln to his good friend Joshua Speed in August, 1855. "We now practically read it 'all men are created equal, except negroes.' When the Know-Nothings get control," Lincoln continued, "it will read 'all men are created equal, except negroes, and foreigners, and Catholics.'" The Know-Nothings were an anti-immigrant and anti-Catholic political party that burst onto the scene in the mid-1850s. In the 1855 state elections, they won striking victories in New York, Pennsylvania, and Massachusetts. The Know-Nothings were "both an expression of the ethnic tensions inherent in mid-century American society," explains historian Eric Foner, "and an attempt by political conservatives to smother the slavery question with a new issue, which could unite Americans of all sections."[25] If the Know-Nothings were to take control, concluded Lincoln, "I should prefer emigrating to some country where they make no pretense of loving liberty—to Russia, for instance, where despotism can be taken pure, and without the base alloy of hypocracy."

Is our democracy a sham? Lincoln's statement should not be taken out of its historical context. In 1855, slavery was the political–economic system in the South, and Franklin Pierce, a pro-slavery Democrat, was President. The nation itself was at boiling point. Five years earlier, Congress had passed the notorious Fugitive Slave Act which required runaway slaves to be returned to their owners—even if the slave was caught in a state or territory where slavery was illegal. Armed conflict had exploded in parts of Missouri and Kansas territory over the slavery question. The Whig party, one of the two major political parties of the time, had recently imploded, and the Know-Nothings seemed poised to take its place center stage. American democracy was bleak when Lincoln

DOI: 10.1057/9781137388117.0006

wrote to Swift. Thus, one might argue that such a question is not relevant at present. At the same time, we have seen that unequal outcomes can persist, and even worsen, over long periods of time. The developments which we explored in the first three chapters of the book and highlighted in this chapter are central to understanding our political system, and thus we should take the question seriously—is our democracy a sham?

In their book *Poor People's Movements: Why They Succeed and How They Fail*, Frances Piven and Richard Cloward argue that representative democracy does not afford the poor, even though a majority, opportunity for change.[26] Why? Because the concentration of wealth overwhelms the electoral–representative system sapping it of free choice. Participation in the political system and one's influence are determined by one's position in society. As long as the lower classes follow the norms that govern the political system, they have little influence. Thus, for Piven and Cloward, the paradox of significant inequality in a democracy is not a paradox. The power of franchise is a façade that conceals the omnipresent control of the economic elite, and the lack of significant redistribution is what one would expect.[27] The only recourse open to the poor is protest. However, "only under exceptional conditions," explain Piven and Cloward, "are the lower classes afforded the socially determined opportunity to press for their own class interests." A sequence or combination of major social dislocations, like those resulting from the Great Depression, must occur "before the anger that underlies protest builds to a high pitch, and before that anger can find expression in collective defiance." Thus, the period of declining inequality in Figure 4.2 is the result of protest stemming from exceptional circumstances and, consequently, represents a deviation from what we would expect normally.

Although a series of major social dislocations might be necessary for progressive change, it does not seem to be sufficient. Juxtaposition of the protests of the 1930s, from which Piven and Cloward base their theory, with the Pullman Strike, the pinnacle of a series of strikes in the early 1890s, illustrates this point. At their climax of almost half a million, striking railroad workers met with unrelenting resistance from George M. Pullman, the owner of the Pullman Palace Car Company; the General Manager's Association, the association of all railroads with terminals in Chicago; and the federal government. Instead of recognition of the right to bargain collectively and a federal agency empowered to uphold that right, which protestors won in the 1930s, the Pullman Strike resulted in the use of blanket injunctions against striking railroad workers, the empowerment of the federal government to act as a strike breaker without the request of the state's governor, and the disintegration of the American Railway Union. Pullman workers did not receive a raise, nor was rent in the town of Pullman reduced, and Eugene V. Debs, President of the striking union, was jailed.[28] Indeed, according to the US Commissioner of Labor, three-fourths of the workers who struck in 1894 never regained their jobs.[29] Thus, the Pullman Strike seems a great contrast to the protests of the Great Depression. Why did strikers not win durable or even transitory gains in 1894? Piven and Cloward's theoretical framework does not provide a clear answer. The Pullman Strike took place during a string of major social dislocations. The Depression of 1893 castrated industry and left millions unemployed. The strike represented a "high pitch" of anger among workers in railroads and supporting industries due to the reduction in work hours and wage, loss of jobs, and increase in intensity of work.

It could be that the lack of durable gains, like the creation of institutions to support unionization, did not materialize because they were not necessary. In the early 1890s, most of the US economy was in its early stages of development in terms of number of workers employed, national scale of company, and capital intensity. However, the Pullman Strike took place in railroads, an industry decades ahead of other US industries in number of workers, scale, and capital intensity. More importantly, there were not even any transitory gains. The inability of Piven and Cloward's theoretical framework to explain these divergent outcomes opens up other questions: does the degree elites work together to promote their cause fluctuate overtime, and, as a result, does elite power also fluctuate? Were elites more cohesive and thus better able to suppress protest in the 1890s than in the 1930s? If they were, how do we explain this fluctuation in elite power?

Another important shortcoming in Piven and Cloward's framework is that the Progressive Era started during a period of prosperity. The nation had seen seven consecutive years of positive real GDP growth averaging 5.4 percent per year when Theodore Roosevelt and Alton Parker began campaigning in 1904. When ballots were cast between William Taft, Theodore Roosevelt, Woodrow Wilson, and Eugene Debs in the 1912 presidential elections, the nation had seen four consecutive years of real GDP growth.[30] However, the "middle class, most of which had been content to accept the conservative leadership of Hanna and McKinley during the period of crisis in the mid-nineties," explains historian

DOI: 10.1057/9781137388117.0006

Richard Hofstadter in his book, *The Age of Reform*, "rallied to the support of Progressive leaders in both parties during the period of well-being that followed."[31] As we have seen in Chapter 3, during this period, laws and institutions were reoriented to arch toward equality. For example, the current income tax was made law in 1913, and surtax rates and the amount of income subject to surtaxes were increased multiple times throughout the remainder of the Progressive Era.

What drove the progressive impulse for reform? It may be that a series of major social dislocations is not necessary or at least that how we understand social dislocation needs to be broadened. Hofstadter explains the Progressive movement as resulting from the change in distribution of wealth, income, and power that took place in the end of the nineteenth century. "In a strictly economic sense," continues Hofstadter, "these men [the Progressives] were not growing poorer as a class, but their wealth and power were being dwarfed by comparison with the new eminences of wealth and power."[32] Others have made similar statements. "[A]n increasing bitterness is felt by a majority which is not worse but better off than before," explained Walter Weyl in his book published in 1912, *The New Democracy*. "This majority suffers not an absolute decline," continued Weyl, "but a relatively slower growth."[33]

Conclusion

How then do we explain the developments looked at in the first four chapters of this book and summarized in Figure 4.2? How do we explain the evolution of the orientation of laws and institutions and income inequality in the United States from the 1870s to the present? Why doesn't the poor majority implement laws that counter the spheres of power in the economic realm or maintain a constant level of redistribution in a political system where they are seemingly empowered? Why are there long periods where the majority seems to be disempowered?

It seems that certain groups are better organized during certain periods to promote desired and block unwanted legislation, and, at other times, other groups are better organized. During the Depression of 1892 and the string of strikes that followed, business was able to successfully resist any unwanted change. In the remaining years of the nineteenth century through the beginning of the twentieth century and during the 1920s, laws and institutions were modified to favor business more and

DOI: 10.1057/9781137388117.0006

more. In the 1930s, things changed. Business was not well organized, and employed and unemployed workers pressed collectively and forcefully for laws and institutions that benefited a broader portion of the population. And, as we have seen in this chapter, substantial change took place via a number of channels: increased protection of collective bargaining, limiting the work week, prohibiting child labor, security for the unemployed, and benefits for those who fought in the war.

These findings are extremely interesting and they open up more questions about the different periods depicted in Figure 4.2. Did business reorganize and come together collectively in the 1970s, 1980s, and thereafter and drive the dramatic change in the NLRA and NLRB we analyzed in Chapter 2? Another important element of this puzzle is that income inequality was a key driver for political activation during the Progressive Era. This forward momentum was squashed during World War I and laws and institutions were made more and more exclusive, but this same motivation drove change during the 1930s. Thus, one must ask: did the reduction in inequality, and thus a relative deterioration of elite's position, spur increased political action in the 1970s, 1980s, and thereafter? How do we put these pieces together to solve the paradox of US inequality? In the next chapter, we will look at another explanation which pulls together the many pieces of the puzzle.

Notes

1 See page 42 on *Hammer v. Dagenhart.*

2 For example, the real value of the federal minimum wage in 2014 is $7.25—significantly below its real value in the 1970s and even more so below its peak in 1968. See US Department of Labor for statistics on the nominal value of the minimum wage (http://www.dol.gov/whd/minwage/chart.htm).

3 Katznelson, I. (2005). *When Affirmative Action Was White: An Untold History of Racial Inequality in Twentieth-Century America.* New York: W.W. Norton. pp. 113–28.

4 In terms of taxation, top marginal tax rates in the United States between 1951 and 1963 were 90 percent. They were decreased in the mid-1960s, but only to 70 percent where they were held, for the most part, through the rest of the 1970s. For data up to 2012, see http://elsa.berkeley.edu/~saez/#income.

5 Office of the Press Secretary, The White House, "Remarks by the President at 'Remembering Franklin D. Roosevelt,' 50th Anniversary Commemorative Services," The Little White House, Warm Springs, Georgia, April 12, 1995,

DOI: 10.1057/9781137388117.0006

cited in Theda Skocpol, "The G.I. Bill and U.S. Social Policy, Past and Future," Social Philosophy and Policy, 14 (Summer 1997), pp. 95–6.

6 Katznelson, I. (2005). *When Affirmative Action Was White: An Untold History of Racial Inequality in Twentieth-Century America*. New York: W.W. Norton.

7 W. E. B. Du Bois, "Du Bois States His Reasons for Backing President Roosevelt," *People's Voice*, October 21, 1944.

8 "Southern Americanism," *Pittsburgh Courier*, November 29, 1940.

9 Robert C. Lieberman, *Shifting the Color Line: Race and the American Welfare State* (Cambridge: Harvard University Press, 1998), p. 7.

10 Katznelson, I. (2005). *When Affirmative Action Was White: An Untold History of Racial Inequality in Twentieth-Century America*. New York: W.W. Norton. pp. 22–3.

11 "To Fulfill These Rights," Public Papers of the President of the United States: Lyndon B. Johnson, 1965. Vol. II (Washington, DC: Government Printing Office, 1966), pp. 635–40.

12 Nixon enforced Lyndon Johnson's affirmative action plan, explains Katznelson, because he wanted "to embarrass organized labor, and enlarge a growing schism between the civil rights movement and white members of unions who might be persuaded to shift their votes to the Republican Party." See Katznelson, I. (2005). *When Affirmative Action Was White: An Untold History of Racial Inequality in Twentieth-Century America*. New York: W.W. Norton. p. 147.

13 Ibid. pp. 147–8.

14 This is not to say that the VRA, CRA, and affirmative action completely leveled the playing field. Indeed, Ira Katznelson's purpose in *When Affirmative Action Was White* is to make a case for continued and more intense efforts to equalize outcomes across race.

15 Vogel, D. (1989). *Fluctuating Fortunes: The Political Power of Business in America*. New York: Basic Books. p. 59.

16 Ibid. p. 67.

17 This paragraph and the following two take considerably from: Stelzner, Mark. 2014. "Political Contest, Policy Control, and Inequality in the United States," *Review of Keynesian Economics*, Vol. 2 No. 3, Autumn 2014. pp. 365–83. Thank you so much to *Review of Keynesian Economics* and Edward Elgar Publishing for releasing the right for republication.

18 Vogel, D. (1989). *Fluctuating Fortunes: The Political Power of Business in America*. New York: Basic Books. p. 146.

19 Ibid. p. 146.

20 Ibid. p. 64.

21 Ibid. p. 62.

22 Edwin L. Dale, Jr, "It's Not Perfect, But It's the Best Yet," *The New Republic*, May 3, 1969, p. 10.

DOI: 10.1057/9781137388117.0006

23 This analysis should not be confused with the business cycle. Whereas the business cycle describes fluctuations in growth, the cycles described here are in regard to economic inequality and government policy.

24 In talking about the nation's commitment to equality, Lincoln was quoting the Declaration of Independence because the only mention of equality in the Constitution, before the Reconstruction amendments, was in "granting each state an equal number of senators." See Foner, E. (1998). *The Story of American Freedom*. New York: W.W. Norton. p. 107.

25 Foner, E. (1970). *Free Soil, Free Labor, Free Men: The Ideology of the Republican Party before the Civil War*. New York: Oxford University Press. p. 196.

26 Piven, F. F. & Cloward, R. A. (1977). *Poor People's Movements: Why They Succeed, How They Fail*. New York: Pantheon Books.

27 Piven, F. F. & Cloward, R. A. (1977). *Poor People's Movements: Why They Succeed, How They Fail*. New York: Pantheon Books, pp. 2–3, 7, 34–6.

28 Lindsey, A. (1964). *The Pullman Strike: The Story of a Unique Experiment and of a Great Labor Upheaval*. Chicago: University of Chicago Press.

29 Taken from Montgomery, D. (1987). "The Fall of the House of Labor: The Workplace, the State, and American Labor Activism, 1865–1925." Cambridgeshire: Cambridge University Press. p. 209.

30 These figures were calculated from Samuel H. Williamson, "What Was the U.S. GDP Then?" MeasuringWorth, 2014.

31 Hofstadter, R. (1955). *The Age of Reform: From Bryan to F.D.R.* New York: Knopf. p. 135.

32 Ibid. pp. 135–47.

33 Weyl, W. E. (1912). *The New Democracy: An Essay on Certain Political and Economic Tendencies in the United States*. New York: Macmillan Co. p. 147.

5
Cycles of Policy Control

Abstract: *In Chapter 5, I put forward another explanation for the mixed performance of our political system in addressing income inequality. This explanation integrates ideas from game theory and behavioral economics and can better explain the long-term trends of the income share of the top 1 percent and the orientation of laws and institutions in the United States since the 1870s.*

Stelzner, Mark. *Economic Inequality and Policy Control in the United States.* New York: Palgrave Macmillan, 2015.
DOI: 10.1057/9781137388117.0007.

A potential answer to this puzzle is that political action for a group good is a public goods game, and individuals exhibit both selfish and group regarding tendencies.[1] Selfish preferences lead to free riding—individuals do not engage in political action.[2] At the same time, group regarding preferences motivate individuals to contribute. However, these preferences are only activated when individuals perceive the system to be unfair in regard to their group. As a result, during some periods, selfish preferences dominate, and, during other periods, group regarding preferences dictate individual action. When selfish preferences dominate, groups are plagued by inaction—no matter their size. On the other hand, when group regarding preferences dominate, a group is able to act collectively.

Let us set aside group regarding preferences for now and focus on selfish preferences and actions that result from them. To be defined as a public goods game for members of the group, political action must be non-cooperative, non-excludable to members of the same group, and the marginal cost of political action must be greater than the marginal benefit. Non-cooperative means that complete contracts cannot be created to bind individuals in the group to specific actions. The act of forging a voting base for a political candidate through protest, donations, or some other form of political action in hopes that the candidate will carry forward some beneficial legislation or block some harmful legislation is not written down in an explicit contract which is permissible in court. A politician can change directions and promote the very legislation supporters thought he would oppose. Past and present, there are ample examples of such actions. Non-excludable means that rewards from political action cannot be excluded from individuals of the group that did not engage in political action. Those workers that did not participate in the crescendo of protests, strikes, and rallies which formed the backbone of support for the New Deal were not excluded from eligibility of benefit from the NLRA, FLSA, and the GI Bill. Evaluating whether the marginal cost of political action is greater than the marginal benefit is more difficult. However, imagine the benefit created by one person staying an hour longer at a protest. In terms of increasing the probability of success of the cause, the marginal benefit is probably very low. At the same time, because the donation of one hour of time is concentrated in that one person, the cost felt by the individual is much larger. Although this brief exploration is not conclusive, I will assume that the marginal cost is larger than the marginal benefit. Thus, political action for a group good is a public goods game, and as a result the best response for selfish individuals is to contribute nothing—i.e. to free ride.[3]

DOI: 10.1057/9781137388117.0007

In terms of political action, the cost of contributing can take many forms. It can be as simple as the amount one donates to a campaign or as risky as participating in a protest or strike which faces repression by private or public authorities. At the same time, the cost of contributing can be the potential loss of one's job in the case that engaging in the political contest runs counter to the employer's interest. I will explore this topic in more depth later. The benefit from engaging in a political contest is the creation of new legislation, change in administration of existing institutions, or change in interpretation of existing laws. This could take the form of a reduction in taxation, more empowering labor laws, or an increase in the amount or redistributive nature of government spending.

As stated earlier, for a selfish individual engaging in a public goods game, the best response is to contribute nothing—i.e. to free ride. However, individuals also exhibit group regarding preferences, behaviors motivated by their perceptions of their group's condition in society. One type of group regarding preference is the strong group fairness motive, where an individual's action is driven by his assessment of the condition of his group relative to what he perceives as fair. The action confers a benefit on members of the group while inflicting a cost on the individual. Thus, if an individual exhibits the strong group fairness motive and perceives the policies of a particular political system as unfair in regard to his group, he will act on the group's behalf even though it is not individually beneficial in a strictly monetary sense.

For a group composed of individuals who exhibit both selfish and group regarding preferences, the more intruding policy is toward the group or the more individuals expect from policy in regard to their group, the greater the total contribution is to the political struggle. Thus, if two groups are fighting over control of the political agenda, all else equal, the group that judges laws and institutions to be more unfair will muster more resources for political action and, as a result, will control the political agenda.

Cost of political action

The cost of political action can take many forms. In some instances, it takes the form of campaign donations. For example, in the campaign of 1896, in efforts to combat the radical threat then embodied in the

DOI: 10.1057/9781137388117.0007

Democratic Party, business and banking interests poured money into Republican coffers. Standard Oil and J.P. Morgan each donated $250,000. The four largest meat-packing houses of Chicago gave $400,000 in total. New York Life Insurance gave "large portions of their clients' premiums." Officially, Republican campaign funds for the election reached $3.5 million. However, counting unofficial contributions their war chest was somewhere between $10 and $16.5 million.[4] In contrast, the Democrats had a "campaign chest of only $650,000."[5] These donations contributed to McKinley's victory. From them, the Republican Party was able to print "120,000,000 copies of 275 different pamphlets in English, German, Italian, Polish, Yiddish, Greek, Swedish, and other languages," and broadcast to millions the speeches of McKinley and those of other prominent party members.[6]

From the late 1970s to the late 1980s, campaign donations were again a very visual cost of political action. Business poured money into political action committees (PACs)—a legal entity created to enable labor unions and corporations to contribute to political campaigns. Within a decade, total contributions to PACs created to further business interests in Congress increased by nearly 500 percent. Although unions also utilized PACs to further their political struggle, total contributions to labor PACs only increased by 50 percent over the same period. As a result, by 1980, corporate PAC donations to political campaigns outpaced union PAC donations.[7]

The cost of political action can take other forms. For example, among laboring groups, it often takes the form of donating time and even risking injury or arrest from actively participating in a protest. The history of the United States is riveted with such instances. For example, on March 6, 1930, international unemployment day, jobless workers in cities across the nation took to the streets to protest their suffering and government inaction. Some of these protests were peacefully received by local authorities. For example, in San Francisco, more than 2,000 unemployed protested without problems. Likewise, in Chicago, over 4,000 unemployed protested peacefully. However, in many cases, authorities were hostile to unemployment demonstrations. In Cleveland, the unemployment protest, which drew 10,000 jobless workers, ended in chaos when a "battle" broke out between the thousands of unemployed and several hundred police officers. The *New York Times* explains that "Scores of men and women were trampled by the charging horses of the police, and more than 100 were injured by flying police clubs during the melee."

DOI: 10.1057/9781137388117.0007

In New York, 35,000 unemployed gathered in Union Square to protest. The rally quickly fell to violence as the demonstrators decided to march on City Hall. The *Times* explains that "an army of 1,000 police, mounted and on foot, supported by scores of detectives, motorcycle men... swinging nightsticks, blackjacks and bare fists, rushed into the crowd, hitting [it out with all]... whom they came in contact... from all parts of the scene of battle came the screams of women and cries of men with bloody heads and faces. A score of men were sprawled over the square, with policemen pummeling them."[8]

Both campaign contributions and participation in a protest represent a cost of political action. In terms of the former, the person or entity that donates incurs a cost—the donation. In terms of the latter, the person that engages in a protest sacrifices her time and potentially much more. Although donating and engaging in a protest are very different, exploring the differences between the two forms of political action would take us too far afield. As a result, for purposes here, it suffices to make a somewhat crude assumption that different types of costs of engaging in political action span a one-dimensional axis which differentiates among magnitudes.

Mobilization

As explained earlier, individuals are not only characterized by selfish tendencies. Many individuals, if not all, exhibit strong group fairness motives. Indeed, I would argue that most of the actions described earlier, whether campaign contributions or participating in protests, are motivated by such preferences. In the example of international unemployment day, it seems more obvious that the actions of protestors could be described as a response to perceptions that the system was unfair in regard to a specific group—unemployed workers or more generally workers. However, it is also the case with elites.

In 1971, Lewis Powell, a Richmond lawyer, former president of the American Bar Association, member of the board of directors of several large corporations, and soon to be Supreme Court Justice, wrote a confidential memorandum to the Chamber of Commerce. In this memo, Powell seems to be calling on businessmen to act collectively because of the unfairness of the system in regard to business. He starts by rebuking the individualistic attitude of businessmen in the past and

DOI: 10.1057/9781137388117.0007

spurs them to act collectively and retake control of politics. "[A]s every business executive knows," explained Powel, "few elements of American society today have as little influence in government as the American businessman, the corporation, or even the millions of corporate stockholders... the American business executive is truly the 'forgotten man.'" Although business was not without power at the time Powell was writing his memo, it was indeed suffering from a series of legislative defeats.[9] "Business must learn the lesson," continued Powell, "that political power is necessary; that such power must be assiduously cultivated; and that when necessary, it must be used aggressively and with determination—without embarrassment and without the reluctance which has been so characteristic of American business."[10]

The political losses from 1969 through the mid-1970s motivated business to overcome its free rider problem and organize to fight against the encroachments of labor and environmentalists in the political realm. Corporations opened offices in Washington and exponentially expanded their lobbying activities.[11] Additionally, businesses created and expanded operations in already existing organizations to push collective issues. The Chamber of Commerce was one of these outlets. Between 1974 and 1980, the Chamber's membership doubled, and its budget tripled. The National Federation of Independent Business was another outlet utilized by business, and, between 1970 and 1979, its membership doubled.[12] The Heritage Foundation served a similar purpose: it was created in 1973 with the intent of "shifting public opinion and policy in a conservative direction." The budget of the Heritage Foundation was pumped up through business donations, and in the early 1980s it was equal in size to that of Brookings Institute.[13]

In 1972, the Business Roundtable, an exclusive organization whose membership was only extended to top CEOs, was created with the purpose of mobilizing "high-level CEOs as a collective force to lobby for the advancement of shared interests." By 1977, it "had enlisted 113 of the top Fortune 200 companies, accounting for nearly half the economy."[14] The Business Roundtable incorporated numerous advantages. For example, members, who were by requirement CEOs, could utilize company resources to fulfill taskforce roles delegated to them. More importantly, their members had special access to government. Thomas Murphy, chairman of General Motors, Irving Shapiro, chairman of du Pont, Reginald Jones, chairman of General Electric, and Clifton Garvin Jr., chairman of the Exxon Corporation, were regular visitors of Jimmy Carter.

DOI: 10.1057/9781137388117.0007

Thus, business had changed by the mid-1970s. Its individualistic actions of the past had given way to collective action to promote the group good. "Most of us went our own individual ways [politically], and when we had problems we addressed them ourselves," explained Thomas Murphy, chairman of GM, of the past decades. "I can remember the days when General Motors didn't have any Washington activities at all. But because of changing circumstances such as Government regulations and other Government activities impacting on our business," continued Murphy, "we find ourselves increasingly involved."[15]

The result

In the mathematical appendix to this chapter, I formally model this dynamic. I assume that individuals form two groups, rich and poor, and that perceptions of fairness, although different for each group, are exogenously given and constant.[16] Inequality is both what each group is trying to control and what spurs individuals to political action. The result is conservative cycles which I display in Figure 5.1. Government policy oscillates between pro-rich and pro-poor. As the poor take control of the agenda, they gradually tilt more and more of the gains from economic activity in their favor. Inequality decreases. However, at some point, the socioeconomic developments ushered in by the pro-poor government lead elites to mobilize. Mobilization eventually leads to elites gaining control of politics and tilting gains from economic activity back in their favor.

Inequality increases. As before, the extension of these policies and increase in inequality motivates the poor to mobilize. Eventually, socio-economic pressures reach a boiling point, and the poor retake control of the government. From this understanding, the answer to the original paradox is that change is gradual, and control in a democracy is not as simple as pure numbers. Before a vote can occur, interest groups have to mobilize to formulate the issues, provide information, encourage turnout, etc. However, this process suffers from the free rider problem. Motivation to overcome the free rider problem derives from activation of group regarding preferences which are conditional on one's perception of the fairness of the system. As a result, control of the agenda and thus positive policy outcomes eventually lead to loss of control. Change in laws and institutions to correct or embrace inequality lead

DOI: 10.1057/9781137388117.0007

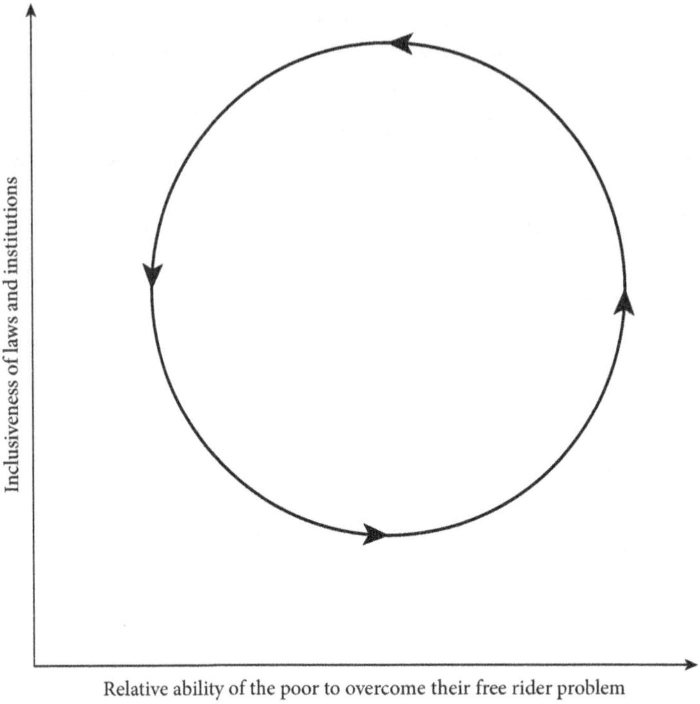

FIGURE 5.1 *The evolution of solidarity and political control*
Source: Author.

to mobilization of the opposing group and, eventually, its ascendance. As a result, government policy oscillates between pro-rich and pro-poor. In turn, inequality oscillates from relatively high to relatively low when policy is pro-rich and pro-poor, respectively.

Comparing with reality

The results described earlier are in general accord with what we found in the first four chapters of the book. In Figure 5.2, I re-present the summary of the evolution of laws and institutions and income inequality in the United States from the 1870s to present. During certain periods, laws and institutions are made more and more exclusive and the income share of the top 1 percent is increasing. This would

DOI: 10.1057/9781137388117.0007

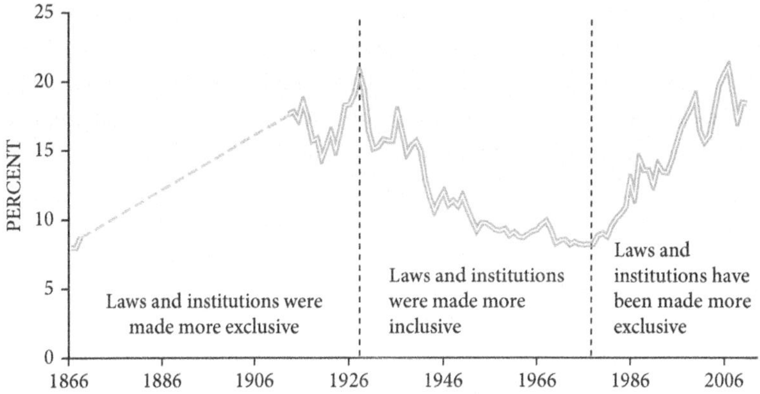

FIGURE 5.2 *Periods in US history—evolution of income inequality and the orientation of laws and institutions*
Source: Author.

correspond to the upper and lower left quadrants in Figure 5.1 and the 1870s through the 1920s and the 1980s to the present in Figure 5.2. During other periods, laws and institutions are made more inclusive and income inequality is decreasing. This would correspond to the upper and lower right quadrants in Figure 5.1 and the 1930s through the 1970s in Figure 5.2.

It should be reiterated that this model only seeks to explain the general trend in the income share of the top 1 percent and the orientation of laws in institutions in the United States and thus leaves out many important issues. For example, race and sectional issues are not examined explicitly. This is a serious omission when talking about politics, laws and institutions, and inequality. Indeed, the political realignments starting in the late 1860s and those of the 1960s involved huge racial components. In the early period, the banner of white supremacy played a large role in goading poor white southerners, many of which originally supported the Radical Republican party, into the Democratic party's conservative embrace. In the latter period, the federal government actions in regard to racial questions in the South played a role in activating new Republicanism.[17] The Taft Hartley Act of 1947 moved in the opposite direction of the New Deal prohibiting certain union activities, and its passage, explains historian Ira Katznelson, was the result of southern discontent about the effects of the NLRA on Jim Crow. Thus, one should not forget that the model is a

DOI: 10.1057/9781137388117.0007

stylized version of history, and in the process of making such a stylized presentation possible, certain factors are left out.

However, some historical developments which might seem incongruent with the model can be explained with a little nuance. The Progressive and the New Era are the best examples of such. As we have seen, from 1900 to 1920, Progressives pushed through an impressive number of liberal laws. Indeed, the current income tax was passed in 1913 via amendment to the Constitution over the Supreme Court's 1895 decision, and in 1916, 1917, and 1919 surtax rates on those at the upper reaches of the income ladder were increased.[18] During the New Era which spanned the 1920s, the many arms of government worked tirelessly to slant the playing fields back in big business's favor. "Never before," explained the *Wall Street Journal* in 1925, "here or anywhere else has a government been so completely fused with business." And the President himself was not shy in agreeing: "This is a business country," explained Calvin Coolidge, "and it wants a business government."[19] Thus, at first glance, the shift in laws and institutions to benefit middle- and low-income groups during the Progressive Era and then the abrupt shift back during the New Era doesn't fit well with the conservative nature of cycles which result from the model presented earlier and formally modeled in the mathematical appendix.

However, the Progressive impulse was exactly the political activation of liberal individuals stemming from group regarding preferences explained in the chapter. The Progressive movement derived from the change in distribution of wealth, income, and power that took place in the second half of the nineteenth century. The Progressives saw the deterioration of their relative position as the result of government policy and sought to right it by changing laws and institutions. The abrupt shift back in the 1920s seems to be a result of the extreme repression of liberal thought during and directly after World War I and the nature of the Progressives themselves. Although they distrusted the very rich, they also did not completely trust those below them. Thus, when President Woodrow Wilson needed support for his war policies, he leaned to the right instead of the left and destroyed the very liberal base that was holding him in power. Indeed, in 1920, Progressive Senator Hiram Johnson of California explained to the press that "The war has set back the people for a generation. They have bowed to a hundred repressive acts... They are docile; and they will not recover from being so for many years. The interests which control the Republican Party will make the most of their docility."[20] As we

DOI: 10.1057/9781137388117.0007

have seen in Chapter 3, laws and institutions were changed dramatically in the 1920s to the benefit of business. This dynamic is not inconsistent with the model presented earlier and in the mathematical appendix below. It can be explained in a less colorful manner as an exogenous increase in the perceived cost of political action for liberal groups.

Thus, despite what is left out and the need to add nuance to explain certain historical developments, this explanation is in general accord with the evolution of both income inequality and the orientation of laws and institutions in the United States. To be sure, the explanation presented here is in harmony with a large body of historical work. In their book *Winner-Take-All Politics*, Jacob Hacker and Paul Pierson explain the secular increase in income inequality since the late 1970s as a result of those at the upper reaches of the income ladder capturing policy control. Another example of historical work which supports the arguments in this chapter is Kim Phillips-Fein's book, *Invisible Hands*. In the book, Phillips-Fein meticulously documents the growth in conservative movements from the beginning of the New Deal to Ronald Regan's Presidency. In the model presented earlier, this is the same as an increase in the activation of group regarding preferences among the rich and thus an increase in solidarity between them. As hypothesized here, this development took place during a period where, in general, laws and institutions favored the rich less and less.

What are the implications of the dynamics analyzed earlier? Are we forever stuck in cycles where the orientation of laws and institutions and level of income inequality fluctuates wildly? How is what we found relevant to addressing our problems at present? To these questions we now turn.

Mathematical appendix

In equation (1), I formalize the general payoff facing a selfish individual engaging in a public goods game:

$$\pi_i = -X_i + \alpha \sum_{j=1}^{N} X_j \tag{1}$$

π_i is the payoff for the ith individual. X_i is the cost of contributing incurred by the ith individual, and $\sum_{j=1}^{N} X_j$ is the summation of the contributions of all N individuals engaging in the public goods game. Some proportion, α, of these contributions accrue to the *i*th individual. For the game to be a public goods game, α has to be less than 1. If this is the case, the best response for the *i*th individual is to contribute nothing.

In equation (2), I formalize the above argument for an individual that perceives taxation to be unfair:

$$\pi_i = -X_i + \alpha \sum_{j=1}^{N} X_j + \beta T X_i \tag{2}$$

Equation (2) is the same as equation (1) except for the last term, $\beta T X_i$. T represents the rate of taxation. X_i is the contribution of the individual, and β is some constant proportion. For a non-zero value of taxation, i.e., $T > 0$, the individual receives a payoff proportional to his contribution from engaging in the political contest. This payoff, encompassed in $\beta T X_i$, should be thought of as a moral or social payoff as opposed to a monetary payoff. Thus, if taxation is high enough, if $T > \frac{1-\alpha}{\beta}$, the best response for the individual, taking into account monetary, moral, and social payoffs, is to contribute to the political contest.

Taking from Daron Acemoglu and James Robinson's paper, "A Theory on Political Issues," I assume that individuals form two homogenous groups: rich and poor.[21] N_R is the number of rich individuals, and N_P is the number of poor individuals. Thus the percentage of the population that is rich is:

$$\frac{N_R}{N_P + N_R}$$

The percentage of the population that is poor is:

$$\frac{N_P}{N_P + N_R}$$

Y_R is the before tax income share of the rich, and $(1 - Y_R)$ is the before tax income share of the poor. Both the number of individuals in each income group and the group's before tax income share are assumed to be constant.

There are two state variables: the tax rate, T, and the frequency of poor individuals engaging in political action relative to frequency of rich individuals, θ. As explained earlier, individuals engage in political action

DOI: 10.1057/9781137388117.0007

because they act on their strong group fairness motive. θ is an accounting term of the relative ability of the poor to overcome their free rider problem. A higher value of θ means that the poor are more organized, and a lower value means that the rich have more successfully overcome their free rider problem. The tax rate is the same for all citizens, rich and poor, and ranges from zero to one (i.e. (0,1)). Once collected, taxes are redistributed evenly among all citizens. Thus the after tax income share of the rich, τ_R, is:

$$\tau_R = \left((1-T)Y_R + \frac{N_R T}{N_P + N_R} \right) \tag{3}$$

The first term is income minus taxes due. The second term is the amount of redistribution per person, $\frac{T}{N_P + N_R}$, times the number of rich people, N_R, which gives the total amount redistributed to the rich as a group. The after tax income share of the poor, τ_P, is:

$$\tau_P = \left((1-T)(1-Y_R) + \frac{N_P T}{N_P + N_R} \right) \tag{4}$$

The first term is income minus taxes due. The second term is the amount of redistribution per person, $\frac{T}{N_P + N_R}$, times the number of poor people, N_P, which gives the total amount redistributed to the poor as a group.

Laws and institutions that affect inequality take place at different points in the production process. Some laws strengthen employers or employees' hand before economic activity takes place and thus affect wages and profits. Indeed, these were the laws we focused on in Chapters 2, 3, and 4. Other laws and institutions redistribute gains from economic activity after income has already been distributed. This construction collapses all laws and institutions that influence distribution, whether or not they operate before or after production, into one policy, taxation, which impacts distribution after economic activity has taken place. The reason for this simplification is mathematical tractability. Thus, a tax rate of zero, $T = 0$, is shorthand for the specific configuration of laws and institutions that best slants gains from economic activity to the rich. In terms of what we have looked at earlier in the book, this would represent configurations like, but more

DOI: 10.1057/9781137388117.0007

extreme than, the 1920s and those at present. A tax rate of 100 percent, $T = 1$, which equalizes after tax income between all citizens, is meant to represent the specific configuration of laws and institutions that most empower the poor. This would represent configurations like, but much more extreme than, those in the 1970s.

I assume that the change in the tax rate, $\dot{T}$, is only a function of θ:

$$\dot{T} = f(\theta) \tag{5}$$

The relative frequency of poor individuals engaging in political action is positively related to $\dot{T}$ (i.e. $\frac{\partial T}{\partial \theta} > 0$). This is because an increase in θ means that the relative number of poor individuals engaging in political action increases and thus the ability of the group as a whole to change laws and institutions, T, in its favor increases. In the 1890s the frequency of poor individuals engaging political action relative to that of the rich was low, i.e., θ was low. As a result, elites were able to resist unwanted political change and slant laws and institutions even more in their favor. Conversely, during the Great Depression, the frequency of poor individuals engaging in political action was high relative to that of the rich, i.e., θ was high, and as a result the poor were able to effectively change laws and institutions (i.e. T).

I assume that the change in relative frequency of poor individuals engaging in political action, $\dot{\theta}$, is only a function of the level of redistribution, T:

$$\dot{\theta} = g(T) \tag{6}$$

The tax rate, T, is negatively related to $\dot{\theta}$ (i.e. $\frac{\partial \dot{\theta}}{\partial T} < 0$). As we saw with Lewis Powell's letter and with business in general, mobilization in the 1970s and thereafter, an increase in the tax rate will increase the frequency of rich individuals engaging in political action. Conversely, as we saw in Chapter 4 with the Progressive movement, a decrease in the tax rate and thus an increase in inequality will increase relative solidarity of the poor and their effectiveness at contesting political control.

Solving the model

Because of its symmetry, the model can be solved explicitly. Algebraic manipulation of equations (5) and (6) yield:

DOI: 10.1057/9781137388117.0007

$$g(T)\frac{dT}{dt} = f(\theta)\frac{d\theta}{dt} \tag{7}$$

All of the terms in equation (7) are functions of time, *t*. Thus, we can integrate both sides of the equation over time. Doing so, followed by a change of variables, yields:

$$\int g(T)dT = \int f(\theta)d\theta \tag{8}$$

Equation (8) can be explicitly solved. Now let us define $H(T,\theta)$:

$$H(T,\theta) = G(T) - F(\theta) \tag{9}$$

$G(T)$ is equal to the integration of $g(T)$ over *T*. Likewise, $F(\theta)$ is equal to the integration of $f(\theta)$ over θ. C is equal to B minus A and thus is also constant. The properties below follow from the definition of $H(T,\theta)$:

$$\frac{\partial H(T,\theta)}{\partial T} = \frac{dG}{dT} = g(T) \tag{10}$$

$$\frac{\partial H(T,\theta)}{\partial \theta} = -\frac{dF}{d\theta} = -f(\theta) \tag{11}$$

$$\frac{\partial^2 H(T,\theta)}{\partial T^2} = \frac{dg(T)}{dT} < 0 \tag{12}$$

$$\frac{\partial^2 H(T,\theta)}{\partial \theta^2} = -\frac{df(\theta)}{d\theta} < 0 \tag{13}$$

As a result of (10) through (13), it follows that:

- $H(T,\theta)$ is convex
- $H(T,\theta)$ has a global minimum in the stationary equilibrium and that $H_T = H_\theta = 0$ holds at equilibrium
- Starting from some initial point other than the equilibrium, the path of (T,θ) will follow level curves corresponding to the constant C (which is determined by the initial values of T_0 and θ_0).

In Figure 5.3, I display the results of equation (5) and (6) and assumptions $\frac{\partial \dot{\theta}}{\partial T} < 0$ and $\frac{\partial \dot{T}}{\partial \theta} > 0$ in the (θ, T) plane. Starting in the upper right quadrant of the graph, the high and increasing level of redistribution threatens the rich and motivates them to mobilize. The familiar problems of free riding and public goods dynamics are swept aside and the resources gathered by the rich for political contestation surge. The horizontal arrow in the upper right quadrant of the graph represents the mobilization of the rich relative to the poor. Otherwise said, it shows that θ is decreasing in this quadrant (i.e. that $\dot{\theta} < 0$). Once $\theta = \theta^*$ (this occurs along the $\dot{T} = 0$ locus), the resources mobilized by each group for the political fight lead to a stalemate. Redistribution doesn't change.

Although not changing, the tax rate is still high enough to mobilize the rich relative to the poor (i.e. θ is still decreasing). This development pushes θ into the upper left quadrant of the graph. In this quadrant, the relative mobilization of the rich is such that they are able to capture the

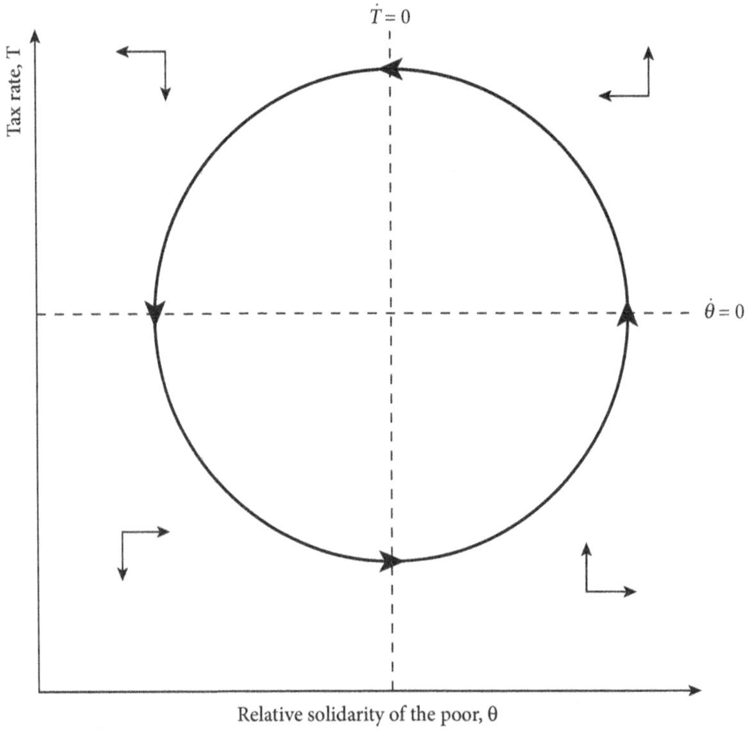

FIGURE 5.3 *The evolution of solidarity and political control*
Source: Author.

political system and gradually shift laws and institutions in their favor. The vertical arrow in the upper left quadrant shows that the level of redistribution is decreasing (i.e. $\dot{T} < 0$). As the rich continue to decrease T, and, as inequality grows, the relative position of the poor is undercut again and again. These dynamics push the system into the bottom left quadrant of the graph.

In this quadrant things are completely reversed from what they were in the upper right quadrant. The low level of redistribution and thus high level of income inequality threaten the poor and motivate them to mobilize. The familiar problems of free riding and public goods dynamics are swept aside and the resources gathered by the poor for political contestation surge. The horizontal arrow in the lower left quadrant of the graph represents the mobilization of the poor relative to the rich. Otherwise said, it shows that θ is increasing in this quadrant. Once $\theta = \theta^*$, the resources mobilized by each group for the political fight lead to a stalemate. The level of redistribution doesn't change.

As before, although not changing, the tax rate is low enough to mobilize the poor relative to the rich, i.e., θ continues to increase pushing θ into the lower right quadrant of the graph. In this quadrant, the poor are relatively more mobilized than the rich and thus are able to take control of the political system and slant laws more and more in their favor. The vertical arrow in the lower right quadrant shows that the level of redistribution is increasing (i.e. $\dot{T} > 0$). As these developments continue, the system is pushed back into the upper right quadrant, and the cycle begins anew.

Notes

1 In this chapter, I take extensively from: Stelzner, Mark. 2014. "Political Contest, Policy Control, and Inequality in the United States," *Review of Keynesian Economics*, 2(3), Autumn 2014. pp. 365–83. Thank you so much to *Review of Keynesian Economics* and Edward Elgar Publishing for releasing the right for republication.

2 By political action, I mean any activity at any stage in the political process that contributes to moving closer to the sought after goal.

3 For information on a public goods game, see: Bowles, S. (2004). *Microeconomics: Behavior, Institutions, and Evolution*. New York: Russell Sage.

4 Josephson, M. (1938). *The Politicos, 1865–1896*. New York: Harcourt, Brace and Co., p. 699.

DOI: 10.1057/9781137388117.0007

5 Sundquist, J. L. (1983). *Dynamics of the Party System: Alignment and Realignment of Political Parties in the United States.* p. 156–7.

6 Josephson, M. (1938). *The Politicos, 1865–1896.* New York: Harcourt, Brace and Co., p. 699.

7 Ibid. p. 121.

8 The *New York Times*, March 7, 1930, p. 3.

9 Vogel, D. (1989). *Fluctuating Fortunes: The Political Power of Business in America.* New York: Basic Books. p. 59.

10 Powell, L. (1971). "Confidential Memorandum: Attack on the Free Enterprise System," August 23, 1971, Powell–Sydnor Correspondence, Powell Papers, pp. 24–5. For a more extensive examination of the growth of the conservative movement in the twentieth century, see: Phillips-Fein, K. (2009). *Invisible Hands: The Making of the Conservative Movement from the New Deal to Reagan.* New York: W. W. Norton & Company.

11 Hacker, J. S. & Pierson, P. (2010). *Winner-Take-All Politics: How Washington Made the Rich Richer—and Turned Its Back on the Middle Class.* New York: Simon & Schuster. p. 118.

12 Ibid. p. 119.

13 Ibid. p. 123.

14 Ibid. p. 120.

15 "Big Business on the Offensive", *New York Times*, December 9, 1979, p. SM34.

16 Indeed, there is solid empirical evidence that the rich and poor do not share common notions of fairness. I will not deal with this explicitly. In the modeling sections, advantages and disadvantages of each group are collapsed into and implicit function.

17 For the racial component of the Redemption movement, see Foner, E. (1988). *Reconstruction: America's Unfinished Revolution, 1863–1877.* New York: Harper & Row. For the racial component of the shift in 1960s politics, see Black, E. & Black, M. (2002). *The Rise of Southern Republicans.* Cambridge, MA: Harvard University Press.

18 *Report of the Secretary of the Treasury*, 1940, pp. 466–79 & 530–3.

19 For *Wall Street Journal* and Coolidge quotes, see Schlesinger, A. M. (1957). *The Age of Roosevelt.* Boston: Houghton Mifflin.

20 For Johnson quote, see Goldstein, R. J. (1978). *Political Repression in Modern America from 1870 to the Present.* Boston: G.K. Hall, p. 167.

21 Acemoglu, Daron and Robinson, James A. (2001), "A Theory of Political Transitions," *The American Economic Review*, 91(4), pp. 938–63.

DOI: 10.1057/9781137388117.0007

6
How Do We Fix It?

Abstract: *In Chapter 6, I use the understanding of the history of laws and institutions, inequality, and our political system to explore some ways to confront inequality at the present.*

Stelzner, Mark. *Economic Inequality and Policy Control in the United States.* New York: Palgrave Macmillan, 2015.
DOI: 10.1057/9781137388117.0008.

On his visits to the United States in the first half of the nineteenth century, French political economist Alexis De Tocqueville contended that democracy was "an irresistible fact, against which it would be neither desirable nor prudent to contend." Political and social forces, predicted De Tocqueville, would eliminate all differences, producing a society of equals.[1] As we have seen, there is no clear long run trend toward equality of income in the United States. Instead, it seems that outcomes oscillate as different groups vie for and take control of policy. At times, democracy works as contended by De Tocqueville. Laws and institutions are made more and more inclusive and income inequality decreases. However, during other periods, like the 1870s through the 1920s and the 1980s to the (?) present, laws and institutions are made more and more exclusive and inequality is increasing. The direction in which policy is molded depends on the relative ability of different groups to overcome their free rider problem. Thus, although it might not be desirable for the population as a whole to disrupt the equalizing power of democracy, we have seen that it is both possible and desirable for elite groups to do so in the United States.

Making durable change

How then do we address the high level of income inequality at present? There are a number of strategies which have been tested and worked. We can take these directly from Chapter 4. For example, empowering collective bargaining or increasing the minimum wage would create counterpoises to employers' monopsony power. As we have seen in Chapter 2, this would have the effect of reducing the difference between what workers produce at the margin and their wage. Income inequality would decrease, and the inequalities that remain would better represent differences in social worth. At the same time, we have seen that changing economic policy is inherently unstable because it leads to change in the political landscape and, ultimately, ushers in economic change in the opposite direction. Consequently, modifying the political system to make it more democratic, and thus removing the possibility of elite reaction as modeled in Chapter 5, is of central importance if we want economic outcomes to be durable.

DOI: 10.1057/9781137388117.0008

Elite control

What factors make elite control possible? The political system in the United States "is among the most opaque, complex, confusing, and difficult to understand," asserts political scientist Robert Dahl in his book, *How Democratic Is Our Constitution*. "If it fails to ensure the fairness promised by the proportional vision, it also fails to provide the clear accountability promised by the majoritarian vision." Of the elements that make our political system comparatively undemocratic, Dahl argues that two of the most important are the strong bicameral legislature which protects state rights through the upper chamber of Congress and the Supreme Court's ability to overturn legislation.

In the United States, each state has two Senators no matter its population. Thus a person who live in states with a relatively small population, or those who donate significantly in these states, have relatively greater representation in the Senate than a person who lives in a more populous state. The purported idea behind the Senate is to protect vulnerable individuals and groups in states with smaller populations. The result of our strong bicameral system has been much different. "Unequal representation in the Senate," remarks Dahl, "has unquestionably failed to protect the fundamental interests of the least privileged minorities." "On the contrary, unequal representation has sometimes served to protect the interests of the most privileged minorities." "Between 1800 and 1860 eight anti-slavery measures passed the House," continues Dahl, "and all were killed in the Senate." As we have seen in Chapter 4, this continued after the Civil War. The South maintained an important veto, via the Senate and other channels, on New Deal and Fair Deal legislation and thus was able to mold laws and institutions to exclude African Americans and protect Jim Crow.

Many Americans have questioned the reason for protecting state rights. "Can we forget for whom we are forming a government?" asked James Wilson, one of the original framers of the Constitution. "Is it for *men*, or for the imaginary beings called *States*?"[2] Although the only mention of equality in the original Constitution is that of equality of representation of states in the Senate, the Reconstruction amendments, the Thirteenth, Fourteenth, and Fifteenth Amendments, were created to remake the Constitution with the aim of putting certain unalienable rights of the individual before the imaginary beings we call states. A century later, the Civil Rights movement further challenged the idea of

DOI: 10.1057/9781137388117.0008

state rights by directly confronting Jim Crow laws. Although these and other movements have made many durable gains, the sanctity of the state as a political entity which deserves political representation and equality in the Senate, even if at the expense of vulnerable minorities and, indeed, sometimes the nation as a whole, has continued.

In terms of the courts, we have seen in Chapters 2 and 3 the important role the NLRB, which is quasi-judicial, and the courts themselves played from the 1980s to present and from the 1870s through the 1920s, respectively, in determining de facto law. Although a strong judicial branch which exercises the right to strike down and reinterpret laws passed democratically by legislature might seem natural to those of us who have grown up under its shadow, its exceptionality quickly becomes apparent when one analyzes other advanced democracies.[3] Among the 16 unitary advanced democracies, explains Dahl, "only about half have some form of judicial review." "Moreover, even among countries where judicial review does exist," continues Dahl, "the extent to which courts attempt to exercise this power varies from the extreme case, the United States, where the Supreme Court sometimes wields extraordinary power, to countries where the judiciary is highly deferential to the decisions of the parliament."[4]

The strength of the judicial branch in the United States is amazing. Based on interpretation of the Constitution, judges, who are not elected, can strike down laws passed democratically by Congress, which is elected. How can this be? "If a law has been properly passed by the lawmaking branching of a democratic government," asks Dahl, "why should judges have the power to declare it unconstitutional?" A number of political movements throughout US history have tried to reform or manipulate the judicial review process. Because of *In re Jacobs* (1885), *Debs v. United States* (1895), *United States v. E.C. Knight Co* (1895) and a number of other detrimental Supreme Court decisions, the Progressives made some effort at judicial reform. And, although not attempting to reform the judicial process, Franklin Delano Roosevelt tried to increase the number of Supreme Court judges in order to tear down the same fortress of judicial decisions which had so tightly constrained the Progressives.[5] However, like the sanctity of the state as a political entity, not much has changed. The judicial branch still holds the power to review democratically passed laws, and it has become more and more active as of late.

These two undemocratic elements of our political system are crucial in magnifying elite representation—making it possible for elites to take control of the political system when they better overcome their

DOI: 10.1057/9781137388117.0008

free rider problem. Thus, in order to make our political system more representative, we could eliminate the upper chamber of Congress and judicial review. The question then arises, is this possible? And, if possible, is it even enough? Indeed, many keen on the subject have had their doubts. Writing both about the 1950s and about the reform efforts of the Progressives, Richard Hofstadter asks: "whether it is possible in modern society to find satisfactory ways of realizing the ideal of popular government without becoming dependent to an unhealthy degree upon those who have the means to influence the popular mind."[6]

During the Progressive Era, the main target for political reform was the machine.[7] The Progressives believed that "[t]he political evils that plagued the country...were not the consequences of deficient organization but of over-organization. The answer to these evils was to move as close as possible to a system of 'direct government' by the people."[8] Through reforms like the direct primaries, popular election of senators, initiatives, referendum, recall, the short ballot, commission government, and franchise for women, the Progressives tried to achieve "direct government." However, they failed.

The Progressives "failed to see that the machine organizations they were trying to destroy did have a number of real functions, however badly they often performed them," contends Hofstadter, "and that any attempt to replace the existing machines had to provide not William Allen White's 'permanent cure'... but rather alternative machines." Extensive organization in the economy and other spheres of life is necessary for a modern society. Thus, if we don't want to turn back the clock but want to address problems that stem from high levels of organization, it is best done through counter organization.[9] At the same time, the Progressives movement failed because it was rife with contradictions. Franchise was simultaneously extended to women in the passage of the Nineteenth Amendment, explains historian Eric Foner, and rescinded from African Americans in the South—starting in Mississippi in 1890 and concluding in Georgia in 1908. Also, literacy tests and residency and registration requirements contracted franchise among the poor in both the North and South.[10] These contradicting actions disempowered constituents who would have been a valuable support base for Progressive change.

During the New Deal, Democrats changed course—empowering unions via passage of the NLRA. After which, northern unions grew quickly and their ability to act as a center of organization to counterpoise business in the economic and political arenas grew in tandem. However, union growth

DOI: 10.1057/9781137388117.0008

was quickly truncated by Jim Crow Democrats nervous that organizing drives in the South threatened their institutions of segregations. In 1947, Republican and Southern Democratic Congressmen joined hands in passing the Taft–Hartley Act over President Truman's veto.[11] As a result, unions never became truly national organizations and thus were unable to reach the point where they represented a complete counter-balance to business.

At present, we might be in a slightly better position than in the past. The Democratic Party largely benefitted from the discontent in the early twentieth century and the 1930s on, and was the national leader of both the Progressive and New Deal movements. However, the party was incredibly compromised due to the desire of its southern bedfellows to further develop and protect Jim Crow laws. Today, the Democrats are a different party, and pursuing a strategy of counter organization via national unions is much more possible. However, if comparing history to the stylized model presented in Chapter 5 tells us anything, it's that although change might be driven by similar motivations and there is potential for identifying some regularity, the form political movements ultimately take can differ dramatically. The Progressives were very different from New Dealers. Thus, it is important to make sure discontent is focused down a path which we know works better—i.e. through positive structures of counter organization.

Furthermore, we have to ask, would elimination of the upper chamber of Congress and judicial review solve all of our problems? This question is definitely difficult to answer given the revolutionary change such actions would represent. However, another glaring factor which reduces the democratic nature of our political system is money. "Senators and representatives, faced incessantly with the need to raise ever more funds," contended Republican Congressman for Arizona, Barry Goldwater, "can scarcely avoid weighing every decision against the question, 'how will this affect my fund-raising?' rather than 'how will this affect the national interest?"[12] Statements like this are ubiquitous. "Across the spectrum, money changed votes," asserted Republican Representative for Florida, Joe Scarborough. "Money certainly drove policy at the White House during the Clinton administration, and I'm sure it has every other administration."[13] And Democratic Senator for New Jersey, Bill Bradley concluded, "We've reached a point where nothing but money seems to matter."[14]

What can be done? In his book *Republic, Lost: How Money Corrupts Congress—And a Plan to Stop It*, Lawrence Lessig argues that we can improve the degree to which Congressmen and other elected figures

DOI: 10.1057/9781137388117.0008

represent the popular will by creating a system of public campaign financing that incorporates choice and the option of limited additional contribution—which is important for tying people to political outcomes.[15] Although Lessig's plan is more practical than elimination of the upper house of Congress and judicial review, it still represents radical change from the system at present. As a result, we must still ask the question, is such change possible? Indeed, is it possible to do all three—eliminate judicial review and the upper chamber of Congress and reduce the influence of money in politics?

Many who have contributed to the literature which recommends significantly changing the political system are cynical about the possibility of realizing this goal. Indeed, it is hard to remain positive as one sees laws and institutions made more and more regressive. However, if we want to address the extremely high level of income inequality in the economy at present and we want changes to be durable, such reforms are necessary. And although they might seem impossible, one must remember that the Thirteenth, Fourteenth, and Fifteenth Amendments would have seemed like a fantasy in the decade before their passage. In 1857, three years before Abraham Lincoln was elected President, the Supreme Court decided in *Dred Scot v. Sanford* that African Americans, even if free, could not be American citizens. The changes that took place in the 1860s would have seemed inconceivable and even ludicrous to contemporaries of the *Dred Scot* decision and other, similarly apocalyptic developments. Likewise, the NLRA, the FLSA, and Social Security also seemed impossible to those that came before them. As we saw in Chapter 3, in 1918, the Supreme Court declared a Progressive law that prohibited child labor unconstitutional "on the grounds that Congress could not use its commerce powers to regulate labor conditions."[16] The severity of this decision—given an estimated 2 million children under the age of 14 were gainfully employed—would have definitely made it difficult to be optimistic. However, change did come, and it will come again. However, this time we are both in a better situation to move forward as a nation, and we have the benefit of knowing what is needed to make change durable.

Notes

1 See Tocqueville, A. (1956). *Democracy in America*. New York: New American Library.

2 See Dahl, R. A. (2001). *How Democratic Is the American Constitution?* New Haven: Yale University Press. pp. 52–3, 115. Many others have made this same point. For example, see Friedman, G. (January 01, 2002). "Success and Failure in Third-Party Politics: The Knights of Labor and the Union Labor Coalition in Massachusetts, 1884–1888." *International Labor and Working-Class History*, 62(1), pp. 164–88.

3 Dahl defines advanced democracies as countries where "basic democratic political institutions have functioned without interruption for... at least a half a century." This includes Austria, Australia, Belgium, Canada, Costa Rica, Denmark, Finland, France, Germany, Iceland, Ireland, Israel, Italy, Japan, Luxembourg, Netherlands, New Zealand, Norway, Sweden, Switzerland, United Kingdom, and the United States.

4 Dahl, R. A. (1998). *On Democracy*. New Haven: Yale University Press. p. 121.

5 Hofstadter, R. (1955). *The Age of Reform: From Bryan to F.D.R.* New York: Knopf. pp. 310–11.

6 Ibid. p. 271.

7 The machine was a political organization ran undemocratically by "bosses" which controlled patronage and distribution of some government services, engaged in propaganda and, at times, other, less law abiding activities.

8 Hofstadter, R. (1955). *The Age of Reform: From Bryan to F.D.R.* New York: Knopf. p. 269.

9 Ibid., pp. 215–71.

10 Foner, E. (1998). *The Story of American Freedom*. New York: W.W. Norton. p. 154.

11 Katznelson, I. (2005). *When Affirmative Action Was White: An Untold History of Racial Inequality in Twentieth-Century America*. New York: W.W. Norton. Also see, Katznelson, I. (2013). *Fear Itself: The New Deal and the Origins of Our Time*.

12 145 Cong. Rec. 25517 (daily ed., October 15, 1999).

13 Schram, M. & Center for Responsive Politics (Washington, DC). (1995). *Speaking Freely: Former Members of Congress Talk about Money in Politics*. Washington, DC: Center for Responsive Politics. p. 89.

14 Bill Bradley, "Government and Public Behavior," Public Talk: Online Journal of Discourse Leadership.

15 Lessig, L. (2011). *Republic, Lost: How Money Corrupts Congress—And a Plan to Stop It*. New York: Twelve. pp. 249–304.

16 See Chapter 3, page 50 (in this book).

DOI: 10.1057/9781137388117.0008

Bibliography

Acemoglu, Daron and Robinson, James A. (2001). "A Theory of Political Transitions," *The American Economic Review*, 91(4), 938–63.

Benartzi, S. and Thaler, R. H. (1995). "Myopic Loss Aversion and the Equity Premium Puzzle," *Quarterly Journal of Economics*, **110**(1), 73–92. (February 01, 1995).

Bernstein, I. (1960). *The Lean Years: A History of the American Worker, 1920–1933*. Boston: Houghton Mifflin.

Black, E. and Black, M. (2002). *The Rise of Southern Republicans*. Cambridge, MA: Harvard University Press.

Blackmon, D. A. (2008). *Slavery by Another Name: The Re-Enslavement of Black Americans from the Civil War to World War II*. New York: Doubleday.

Bowles, S. (2004). *Microeconomics: Behavior, Institutions, and Evolution*. New York: Russell Sage.

Bronfenbrenner, K. (2009). "No Holds Barred: The Intensification of Employer Opposition to Organizing," Economic Policy Institute Briefing Paper No. 235 (May 30, 2009).

Bruce, R. V. (1959). *1877: Year of Violence*. Indianapolis: Bobbs-Merrill.

Carnegie, Andrew (1906). "The Gospel of Wealth," *The North American Review*, 183(599) (September 21, 1906).

Dahl, R. A. (1998). *On Democracy*. New Haven: Yale University Press.

Dahl, R. A. (2001). *How Democratic Is the American Constitution?* New Haven: Yale University Press.

David, H. (1958). *The History of the Haymarket Affair: A Study in the American Social-Revolutionary and Labor Movements*. New York: Russell & Russell.

Fairman, C. (July 01, 1953). "The So-Called Granger Cases, Lord Hale, and Justice Bradley." *Stanford Law Review*, 5(4), 587–679.

Fine, S. (1956). *Laissez Faire and the General-Welfare State: A Study of Conflict in American Thought, 1865–1901*. Ann Arbor: University of Michigan Press.

Fishback, P. V., Holmes, R., and Allen, S. (January 01, 2009). "Lifting the Curse of Dimensionality: Measures of the States' Labor Legislation Climate in the United States during the Progressive Era." *Labor History*, 50(3).

Foner, E. (1970). *Free Soil, Free Labor, Free Men: The Ideology of the Republican Party before the Civil War*. New York: Oxford University Press.

Foner, E. (1988). *Reconstruction: America's Unfinished Revolution, 1863–1877*. New York: Harper & Row.

Foner, E. (1998). *The Story of American Freedom*. New York: W.W. Norton.

Forbath, W. E. (1991). *Law and the Shaping of the American Labor Movement*. Cambridge, MA: Harvard University Press.

Friedman, G. (1999). *State-Making and Labor Movements: France and the United States, 1876–1914*. Ithaca, New York: Cornell University Press.

Friedman, G. (2002). "Success and Failure in Third-Party Politics: The Knights of Labor and the Union Labor Coalition in Massachusetts, 1884–1888." *International Labor and Working-Class History*, 62(1), 164–88. (January 01, 2002).

Goldin, C. D. and Katz, L. F. (2008). *The Race between Education and Technology*. Cambridge, MA: Belknap Press of Harvard University Press.

Goldstein, R. J. (1978). *Political Repression in Modern America from 1870 to the Present*. Boston: G.K. Hall.

Gould, W. B. (2000). *Labored Relations: Law, Politics, and the NLRB—A Memoir*. Cambridge, MA: MIT Press.

Hacker, J. S. and Pierson, P. (2010). *Winner-Take-All Politics: How Washington Made the Rich Richer—And Turned Its Back on the Middle Class*. New York: Simon & Schuster.

Hofstadter, R. (1955). *The Age of Reform: From Bryan to F.D.R.* New York: Knopf.

DOI: 10.1057/9781137388117.0009

Josephson, M. (1938). *The Politicos, 1865–1896*. New York: Harcourt, Brace and Co.

Kahneman, D., Slovic, P. and Tversky, A. (1982). *Judgment under Uncertainty: Heuristics and Biases*. Cambridge: Cambridge University Press.

Katznelson, I. (2005). *When Affirmative Action Was White: An Untold History of Racial Inequality in Twentieth-Century America*. New York: W.W. Norton.

Katznelson, I. (2013). *Fear Itself: The New Deal and the Origins of Our Time*.

Krugman, P. R. (2012). *End This depression Now!* New York: W.W. Norton & Company.

Lessig, L. (2011). *Republic, Lost: How Money Corrupts Congress—And a Plan to Stop It*. New York: Twelve.

Leuchtenburg, W. E. (1958). *The Perils of Prosperity, 1914–32*. Chicago: University of Chicago Press.

Lieberman, Robert C. (1998). *Shifting the Color Line: Race and the American Welfare State*. Cambridge: Harvard University Press.

Lindsey, A. (1964). *The Pullman Strike: The Story of a Unique Experiment and of a Great Labor Upheaval*. Chicago: University of Chicago Press.

Manning, A. (2003). *Monopsony in Motion: Imperfect Competition in Labor Markets*. Princeton, NJ: Princeton University Press.

McMurry, Donald L. (1961). "The Legal Ancestry of the Pullman Strike Injunctions," *Industrial and Labor Relations Review*, 14(2) (January 1961), 235–56.

Montgomery, D. (1987). *The Fall of the House of Labor: The Workplace, the State, and American Labor Activism, 1865–1925*. Cambridgeshire: Cambridge University Press.

Okun, A. M. (1975). *Equality and Efficiency, the Big Tradeoff*. Washington: Brookings Institution.

Paul, A. M. (1960). *Conservative Crisis and the Rule of Law: Attitudes of Bar and Bench, 1887–1895*. Ithaca, NY: Published for the American Historical Association [by] Cornell University Press.

Phillips-Fein, K. (2009). *Invisible Hands*. New York: W. W. Norton & Company.

Piketty, T. and Goldhammer, A. (2014). *Capital in the Twenty-First Century*.

DOI: 10.1057/9781137388117.0009

Piketty, Thomas and Saez, Emmanuel (2003). "Income Inequality in the United States, 1913–1998," *The Quarterly Journal of Economics*, 118(1), 1–39.

Piven, F. F. and Cloward, R. A. (1977). *Poor People's Movements: Why They Succeed, How They Fail.* New York: Pantheon Books.

Powell, L. (1971). "Confidential Memorandum: Attack on the Free Enterprise System," August 23, 1971, Powell-Sydnor Correspondence, Powell Papers.

Ratner, S. (1942). *American Taxation: Its History as a Social Force in Democracy*. New York: W.W. Norton & Company.

Roche, J. P. (1963). "Entrepreneurial Liberty and the Fourteenth Amendment." *Labor History*, 4(1), 3–31. (January 01, 1963).

Schlesinger, A. M. (1957). *The Age of Roosevelt*. Boston: Houghton Mifflin.

Schram, M. and Center for Responsive Politics (Washington, DC). (1995). *Speaking Freely: Former Members of Congress Talk about Money in Politics*. Washington, DC: Center for Responsive Politics.

Scott, T. A. (1877). "The Recent Strikes." *The North American Review*,125(258), 351–62. (September 01, 1877).

Soule, G. H. (1947). *Prosperity Decade: From War to Depression: 1917–1929*. New York: Rinehart.

Stelzner, M. (2014). "Political Contest, Policy Control, and Inequality in the United States," *Review of Keynesian Economics*, 2(3), Autumn 2014, 365–83.

Stelzner, M. (2014a). "Income Inequality in the United States in the Late 1860s," working paper.

Sundquist, J. L. (1983). *Dynamics of the Party System: Alignment and Realignment of Political Parties in the United States*. Washington: The Brookings Institution.

Theda Skocpol (1997). "The G.I. Bill and U.S. Social Policy, Past and Future," *Social Philosophy and Policy*, 14 (Summer 1997), pp. 95–6.

Tocqueville, A. (1956). *Democracy in America*. New York: New American Library.

United States. (1975). Historical Statistics of the United States: Colonial Times to 1970. Washington: US Dept. of Commerce, Bureau of the Census.

Vogel, D. (1989). *Fluctuating Fortunes: The Political Power of Business in America*. New York: Basic Books.

DOI: 10.1057/9781137388117.0009

Wages and Human (2009). Capital in the U.S. Financial Industry: 1909–2006, Thomas Philippon and Ariell Reshef. NBER Working Paper No. 14644.

Weyl, W. E. (1912). *The New Democracy: An Essay on Certain Political and Economic Tendencies in the United States*. New York: Macmillan Co.

Williamson, Samuel H. (2013). "What Was the U.S. GDP Then?" *MeasuringWorth*, August 2013. http://www.measuringworth.com/datasets/usgdp/result.php.

Wilson, W. and Hale, W. B. (1913). *The New Freedom: A Call for the Emancipation of the Generous Energies of a People*. New York: Doubleday, Page & Company.

Witte, E. E. (1969). *The Government in Labor Disputes*. New York: Arno.

Woodward, C. V. (1951). *Origins of the New South, 1877–1913*. Baton Rouge: Louisiana State University Press.

DOI: 10.1057/9781137388117.0009

Index

DOI: 10.1057/9781137388117.0010

DOI: 10.1057/9781137388117.0010

DOI: 10.1057/9781137388117.0010